MATHS
GAMES
FOR
BRIGHT
SPARKS

Puzzles and solutions by
Dr Gareth Moore
B.Sc (Hons) M.Phil Ph.D

Illustrations by Jess Bradley

Designed by Zoe Bradley

Edited by Sue McMillan and Susannah Bailey

Cover design by Angie Allison

MATHS GAMES
FOR
BRIGHT SPARKS

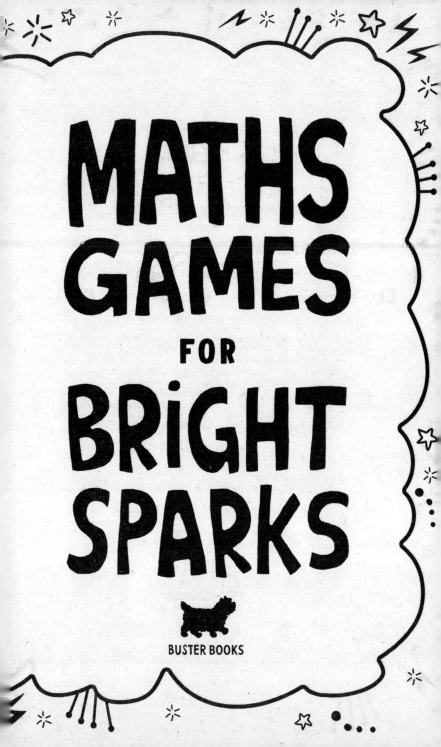

BUSTER BOOKS

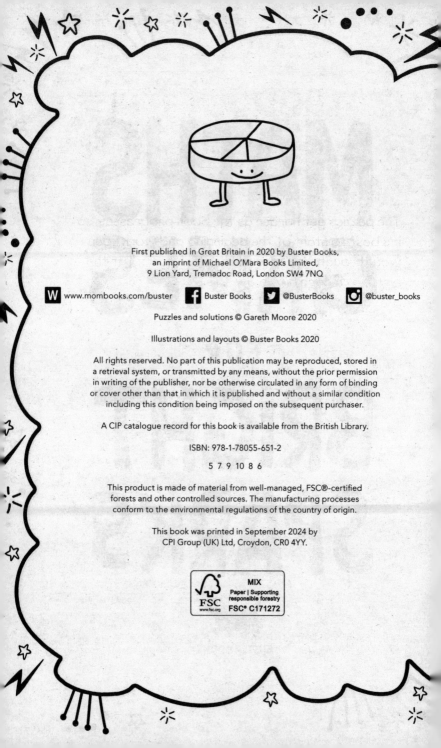

First published in Great Britain in 2020 by Buster Books,
an imprint of Michael O'Mara Books Limited,
9 Lion Yard, Tremadoc Road, London SW4 7NQ

W www.mombooks.com/buster   f Buster Books   🐦 @BusterBooks   📷 @buster_books

Puzzles and solutions © Gareth Moore 2020

Illustrations and layouts © Buster Books 2020

A CIP catalogue record for this book is available from the British Library.

ISBN: 978-1-78055-651-2

5 7 9 10 8 6

This product is made of material from well-managed, FSC®-certified
forests and other controlled sources. The manufacturing processes
conform to the environmental regulations of the country of origin.

This book was printed in September 2024 by
CPI Group (UK) Ltd, Croydon, CR0 4YY.

MIX
Paper | Supporting
responsible forestry
FSC® C171272

INTRODUCTION

This book is packed with more than 80 amazing maths games to challenge your brain. Are you ready to tackle them?

The puzzles get harder as the book progresses, so it's best to start at the beginning and work your way through. You'll see a little clock symbol at the bottom of each puzzle. Use this space to record how long each game takes you to complete.

There's plenty of space on the pages to make notes as you go, but if you need more room to work out your answers, use the blank pages at the back of the book.

The instructions for each maths game will tell you how to get started. If you're not sure what to do, read them again in case there is something you've missed. Many of the maths games also include a finished example that will help you along the way.

Use a pencil to fill in your answers, then you can change them if you need to.

If you are still stuck, you could also try asking a grown-up. If you're *really* stuck, have a peek at the answers in the back of the book, and then try and work out how you could have got to that solution yourself.

Good luck and have fun!

Introducing the Maths Games Master:
Gareth Moore, B.Sc (Hons) M.Phil Ph.D

Dr Gareth Moore is an Ace Puzzler and author of many puzzle and maths books.

He created online brain-training site BrainedUp.com, and runs the online puzzle site PuzzleMix.com. Gareth has a Ph.D from the University of Cambridge, where he taught machines to understand spoken English.

ROBOT BUDDIES

1

Each of these robots has a number. Can you draw lines to sort them into pairs, so each robot is joined to another whose number is twice (2x) their value?

One pair has been joined already: 3 x 2 = 6, so robot 3 has been paired with robot 6.

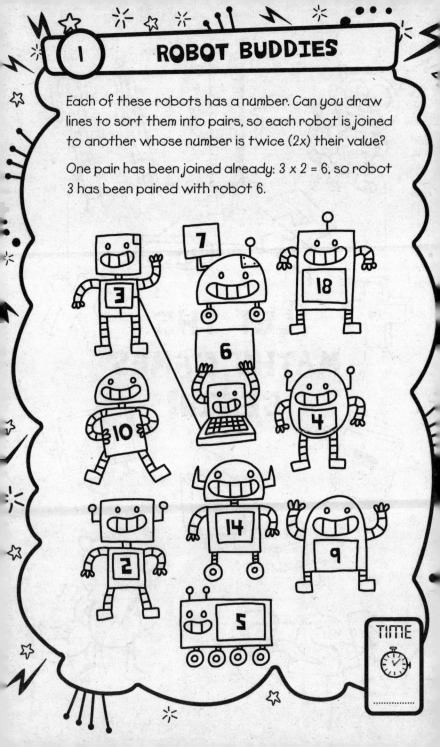

TIME

The picture below has been made by drawing three overlapping shapes. What are those three shapes?

....

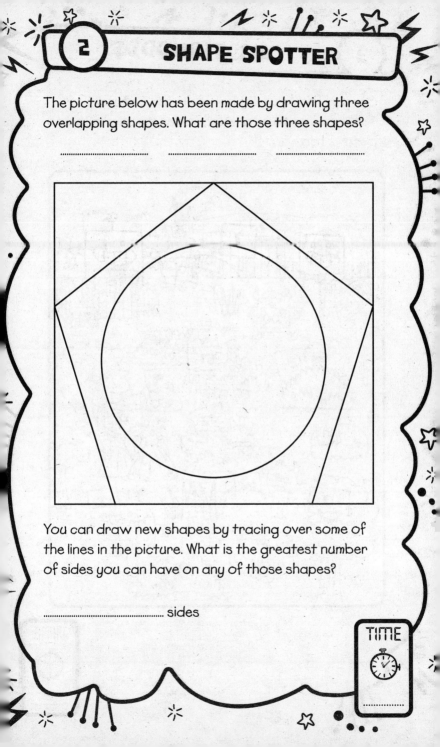

You can draw new shapes by tracing over some of the lines in the picture. What is the greatest number of sides you can have on any of those shapes?

.... sides

TIME

ALL THE ODDS

Can you find ten odd numbers in this picture? Take care, as there are some even numbers in the picture, too.

TIME

4 MILKSHAKE MATHS

Here are five numbered milkshakes. Choose milkshakes for each tray so that they add up to the number shown on it. You can use each milkshake only once on each tray.

EXAMPLE:

1. 11
2. 14
3. 16
4. 25

TIME
....

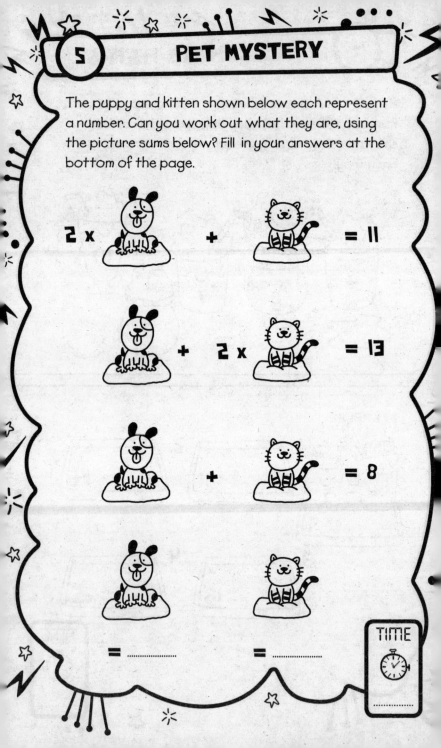

PET MYSTERY

The puppy and kitten shown below each represent a number. Can you work out what they are, using the picture sums below? Fill in your answers at the bottom of the page.

2 x 🐶 + 🐱 = 11

🐶 + 2 x 🐱 = 13

🐶 + 🐱 = 8

🐶 = ... 🐱 = ...

TIME

MAZE MASTER

Help the monster slug find the path home through the maze. When you reach her house, go back to the start and add up just the numbers on the path. Write your answer in the space below.

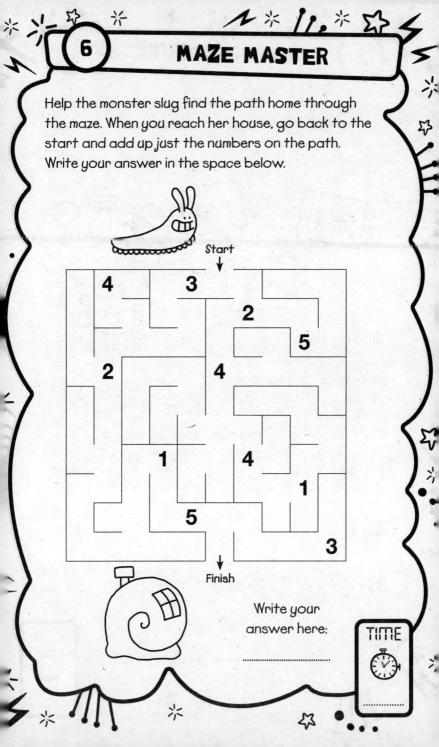

Start

4   3

2

5

2   4

1   4

1

5

3

Finish

Write your answer here:

....

TIME

SUPER SEQUENCES

Can you match each of the three number sequences below with the correct instruction card?

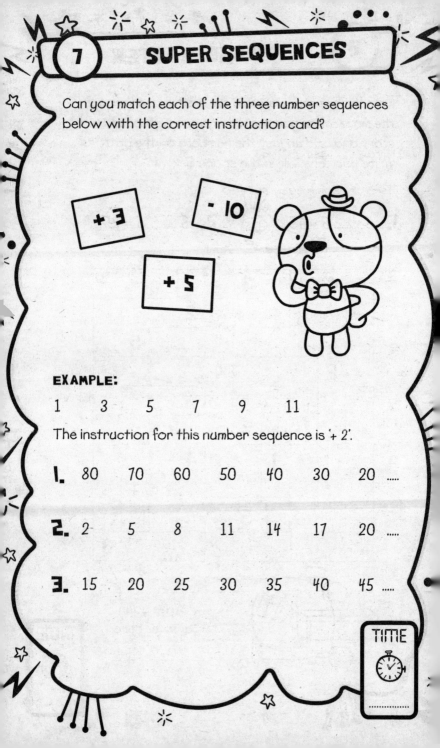

+ 3

- 10

+ 5

EXAMPLE:

1   3   5   7   9   11

The instruction for this number sequence is '+ 2'.

1. 80   70   60   50   40   30   20 .....

2. 2   5   8   11   14   17   20 .....

3. 15   20   25   30   35   40   45 .....

TIME

....

MISSING SIGNS

Write in the signs missing from these calculations so that each one is correct. You can choose from:

+   **-**   **X**   **÷**

Here are some easy ones to start with:

1. 3 .... 5 = 15

2. 5 .... 5 = 25

3. 4 .... 8 = 12

4. 20 .... 2 = 10

Now have a go at these trickier ones:

5. 19 .... 19 = 38

6. 35 .... 5 = 7

7. 87 .... 13 = 100

8. 99 .... 12 = 87

9. 5 .... 5 = 0

10. 11 .... 10 = 110

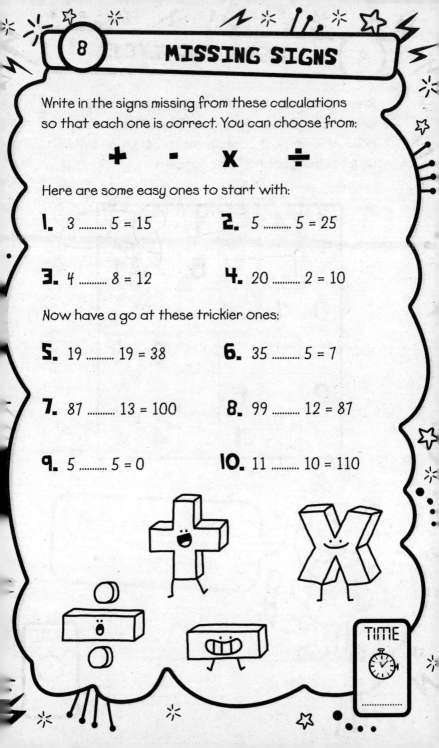

TIME

....

Place the numbers 1 to 6 so they appear once each in every row and column. To make it easier, grey squares must contain even numbers and white squares must contain odd numbers.

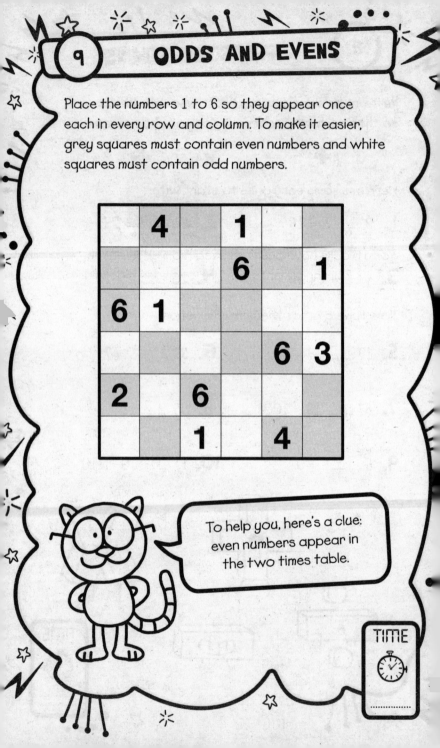

To help you, here's a clue: even numbers appear in the two times table.

TIME

COUNTING CUBES

In this example, eight blocks are arranged in a 2 x 2 x 2 cube.

EXAMPLE:

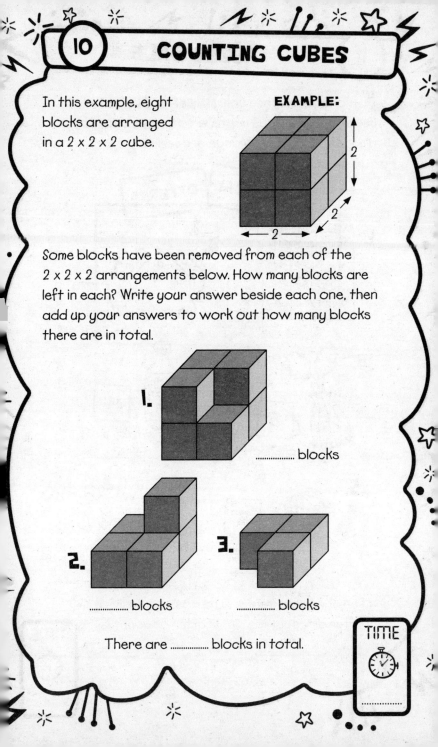

Some blocks have been removed from each of the 2 x 2 x 2 arrangements below. How many blocks are left in each? Write your answer beside each one, then add up your answers to work out how many blocks there are in total.

1.

.... blocks

2.

.... blocks

3.

.... blocks

There are .... blocks in total.

TIME

....

ALIEN SALE

On planet Zork, the supermarket is having a sale. Use your marvellous maths skills to work out the discount on these strange groceries.

SPECIAL OFFERS!

I. 6 take ½ off

....

2. 4 take ¼ off

....

3. 6 take ⅓ off

....

4. 4 take ½ off

....

5. 9 take ⅓ off

....

The cheapest item after discount is:

....

The most expensive item after discount is:

....

TIME

....

NUMBER PATHS

Place a number from 1 to 16 into each empty square, so no number repeats within the puzzle. The numbers must form a path from 1 to 16, moving from square to square in any direction except diagonally.

EXAMPLE:

10	9	8	1
11	12	7	2
16	13	6	3
15	14	5	4

1.

	16	11	
14			9
5			8
	3	2	

2.

	9	14	
	8	7	

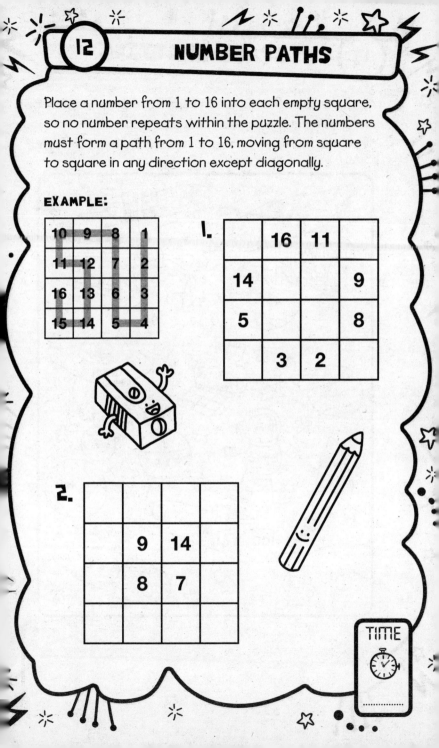

TIME

SPACE SPOTTING

All of the sums that are in the same position on these two pictures have the same answer, apart from five. Can you circle the five sums whose answers have been changed?

Once you have found the five different sum results, can you also find five differences between the two pictures?

SUPER SUDOKU

Use your skills to fill in the sudoku puzzles opposite. Place the numbers 1 to 4 so they appear once each in every row, column and bold-lined 2 x 2 area. The numbers outside the grid are the sum of the nearest two numbers in that row or column.

In the circled area, notice how the 6 clue is solved by the 2 and 4, since 6 = 2 + 4.

EXAMPLE:

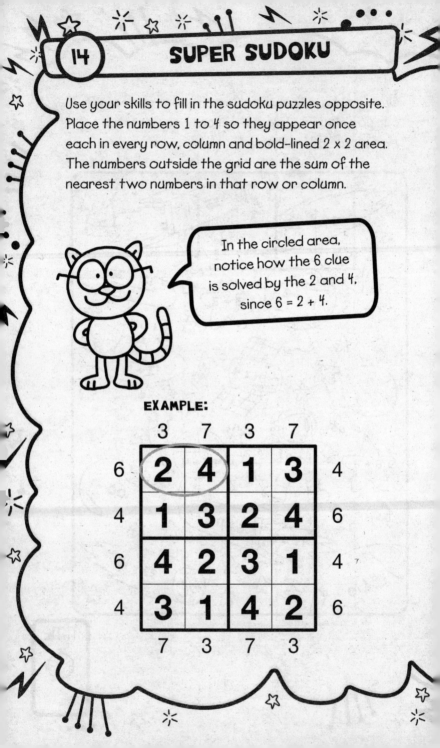

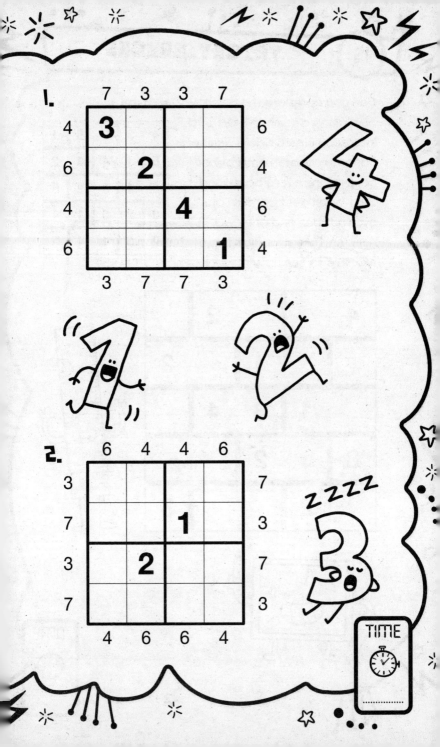

Can you complete the brick wall by placing a number from 1 to 5 into each empty brick? Numbers cannot repeat in any row or column, and every bold-lined 2 x 1 brick must contain one even number and one odd number. Take a look at the example to see how it works.

EXAMPLE:

4	3	2	5	1
5	1	4	3	2
1	4	3	2	5
3	2	5	1	4
2	5	1	4	3

4			2	
		1		2
	1	3	4	
3		2		
	2			3

2x1

TIME

TWO AWAY SQUARE

Can you place the numbers 1 to 4 so they appear once each in every row and column? If two squares have a bar between them, the numbers must have a difference of 2. One pair of these numbers is circled in the example – notice how 3 – 1 = 2.

EXAMPLE:

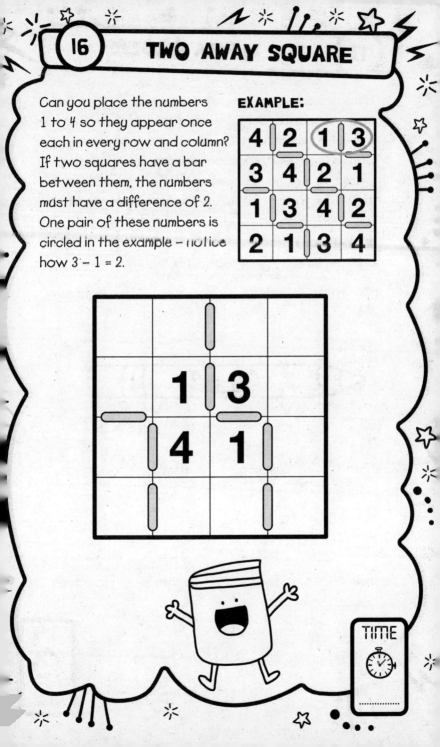

TIME

ALPHA ORDER

Here are some numbers, written in words. Sort them into numerical order by writing the letters 'A' (for the lowest number) to 'H' (for the highest) on the lines above them. Next, sort the words into alphabetical order by writing the numbers '1' (for the first letter) to '8' (for the last letter) on the lines below them.

EXAMPLE:

B	D	A	C
twelve	ninety	six	eighteen
4	2	3	1

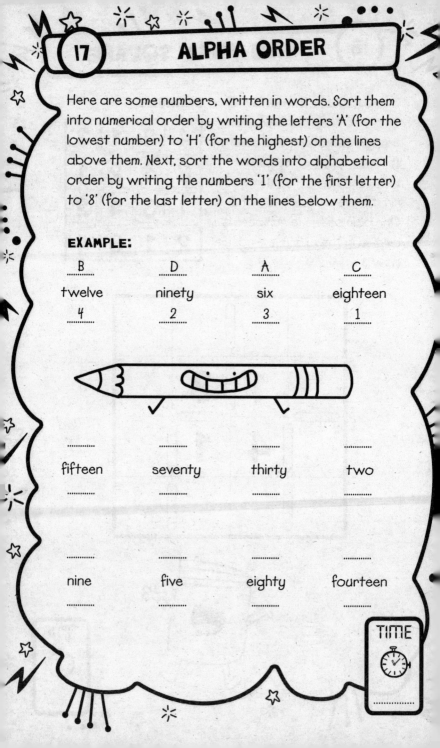

fifteen	seventy	thirty	two

nine	five	eighty	fourteen

TIME

SEQUENCE SOLVER

Can you work out which number (or numbers) should come next in each of the following mathematical sequences?

EXAMPLE:

2   4   6   8   10   12   <u>14</u>

1. 4   7   10   13   16   19   ....

2. 55   50   45   40   35   30   ....

3. 99   88   77   66   55   44   ....

4. 78   90   102   114   126   ....

TIME

NUMBER PYRAMIDS

Fill in the empty blocks to complete these pyramids. Each block must equal the sum of the numbers on the two blocks directly beneath it.

In the example, the 20 block is the sum of the 12 and 8 beneath it, which have been circled.

EXAMPLE:

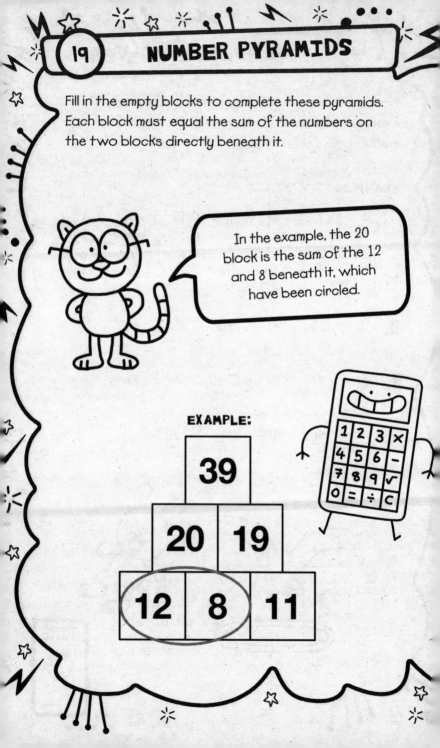

39

20   19

12   8   11

1.

7	8	15

2.

	13	
12		7

TIME

SHAPE SUMS

Can you solve each of these shape calculations? To work out each total, replace each shape with the number of sides that it has.

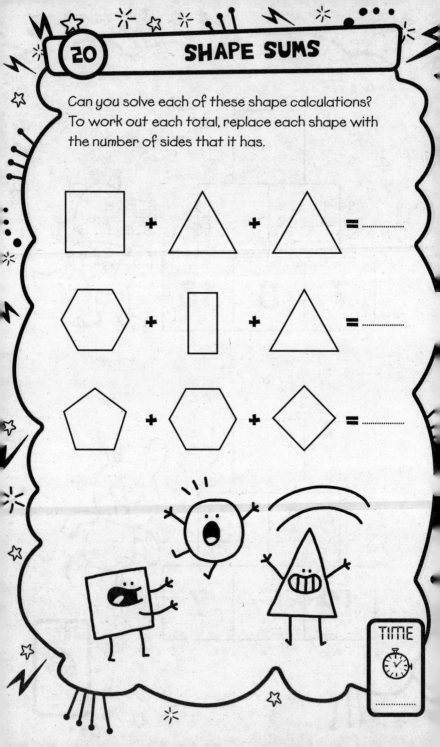

TOUCHY NUMBERS

Complete this puzzle by writing a number from 1 to 6 in every empty square, so no number repeats within any row or column. No two touching squares – including diagonally touching squares – can contain the same number.

EXAMPLE:

1	2	5	3	4	6
3	6	4	2	5	1
2	5	1	6	3	4
6	4	3	5	1	2
5	1	2	4	6	3
4	3	6	1	2	5

3					1
	5	1	2	3	
	1	2	4	6	
6					5

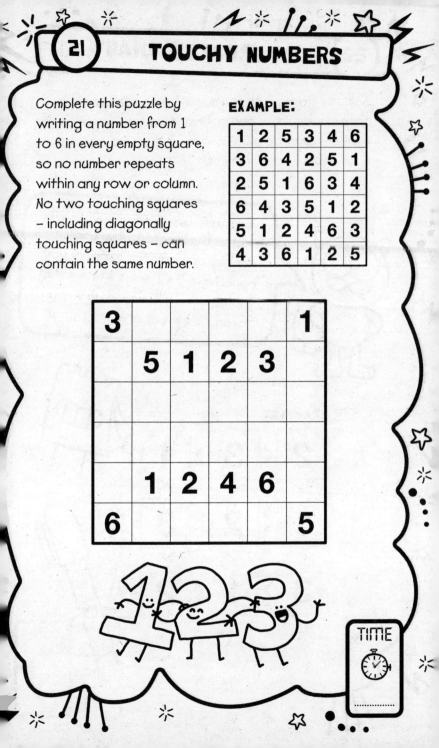

TIME

Fill in the grids so the numbers 1 to 3 appear once in every row and column. Here's the catch – numbers must be placed so that all of the 'greater than' signs (>) are correct.

Greater than signs always point from the bigger to the smaller number of a pair. For example, you could have '3 > 1' since 3 is greater than 1, but '1 > 3' would be wrong because 1 is not greater than 3.

EXAMPLE:

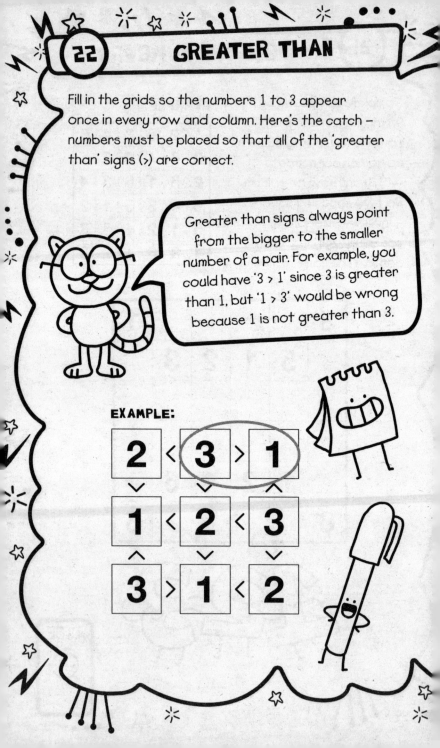

2	<	3	>	1
∨		∨		∧
1	<	2	<	3
∧		∨		∨
3	>	1	<	2

It's time to turn detective! How many rectangles can you spot in the shape below? Look closely - the rectangles differ in size and some may overlap, too. Don't forget to include the large one all around the outside.

Write your answer here:

.... rectangles

TIME

....

DAY DECIDER

Are you a whizz with the days of the week?
Work out the answers to these calendar challenges.

1. If today is Thursday, what day of the week will it be in 10 days' time?

....

2. The day after tomorrow is Sunday, so what day is it today?

....

3. If the day before yesterday was five days before Thursday, then what day is it today?

....

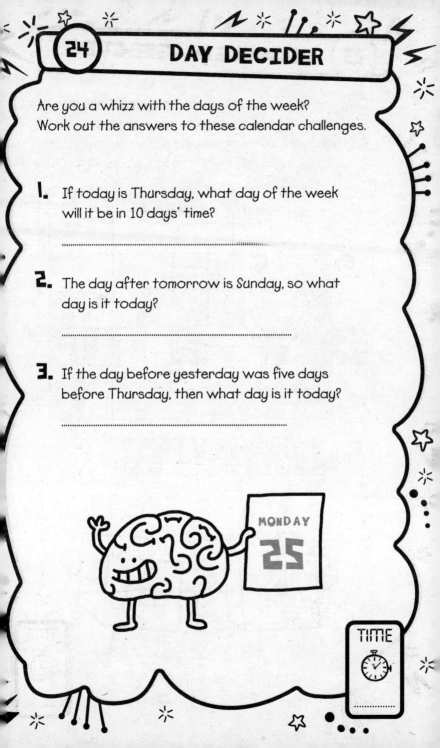

MONDAY
25

TIME

Only one of these shapes can be folded along the black lines to make a complete, six-sided cube. Can you work out which one it is?

A.

B.   C.

D.

E.

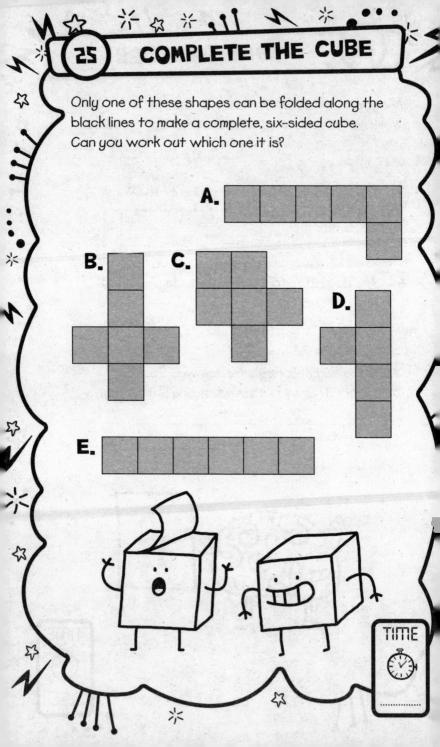

TIME

Draw along the dashed lines to divide the grid up into a set of rectangles, with one number per rectangle. Each number must end up inside a rectangle of that exact number of grid squares. For example, the 12 in the example is inside a 12-square rectangle.

EXAMPLE:

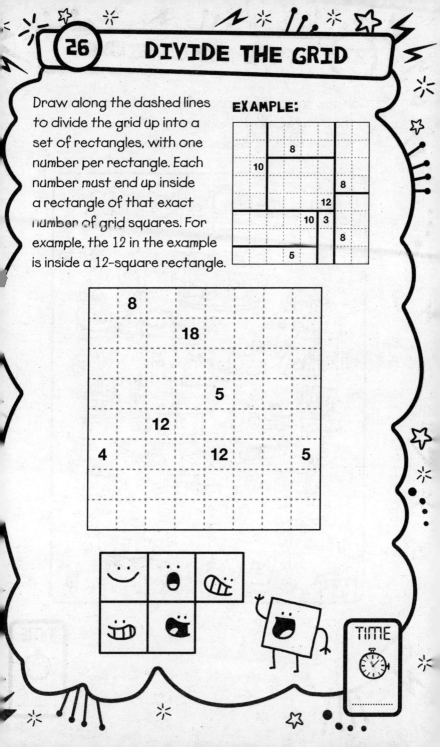

Can you find eight numbers from the five times table in the picture below? Take care – other numbers not in the five times table are shown, too.

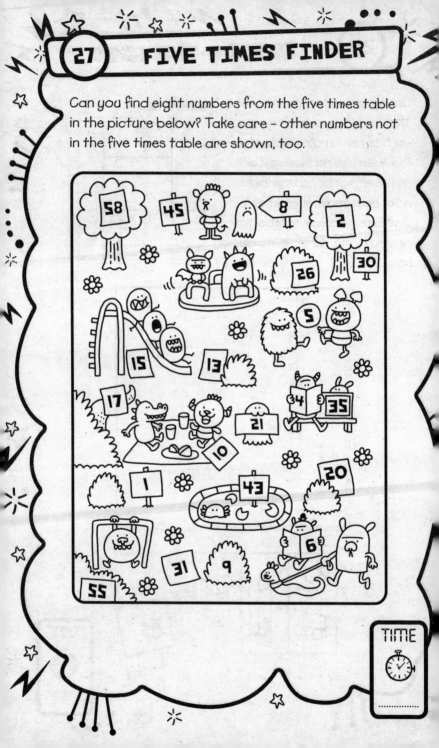

TIME

TWICE AS TRICKY

Can you place the numbers 1 to 5 so they appear once each in every row and column? If two squares have a bar between them, the numbers must have a difference of 2. One pair of these numbers is circled in the example – notice how 5 – 3 = 2.

EXAMPLE:

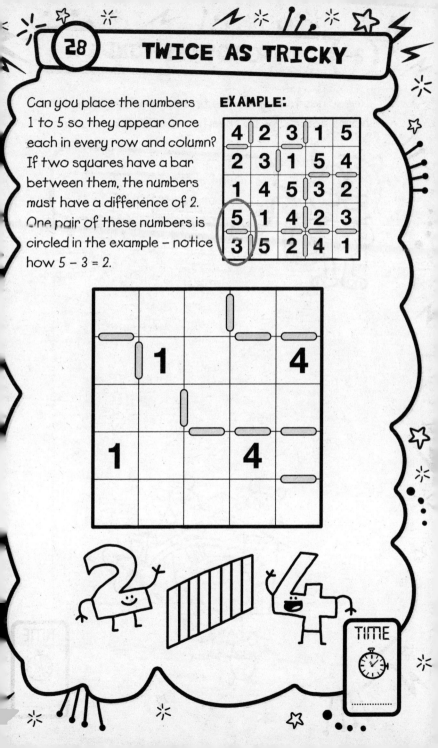

GOOD TIMING

Draw lines to pair up the times that are exactly six hours apart. One of them has been done for you.

Some of the times are a.m. and some are p.m.

5 p.m.

10 p.m.

9 p.m.

7 a.m.

1 a.m.

3 a.m.

4 a.m.

6 a.m.

11 p.m.

2 p.m.

8 p.m.

12 p.m.

TIME

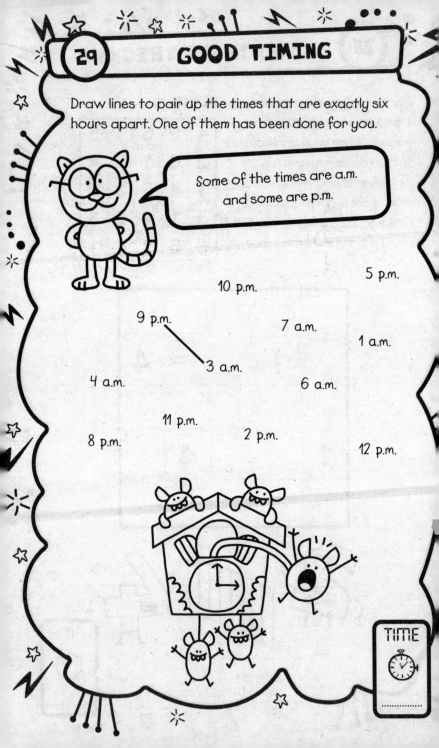

BUDDY UP

Each of these monsters has a number. Can you draw lines to sort them into pairs, so each monster is joined to another whose number is three times their value?

NUMBER DARTS

Complete the sums below by choosing one number from the inner ring and one number from the outer ring of the dartboard to make each total. For example, you could get a total of 13 by picking 3 from the inner ring and 10 from the outer ring.

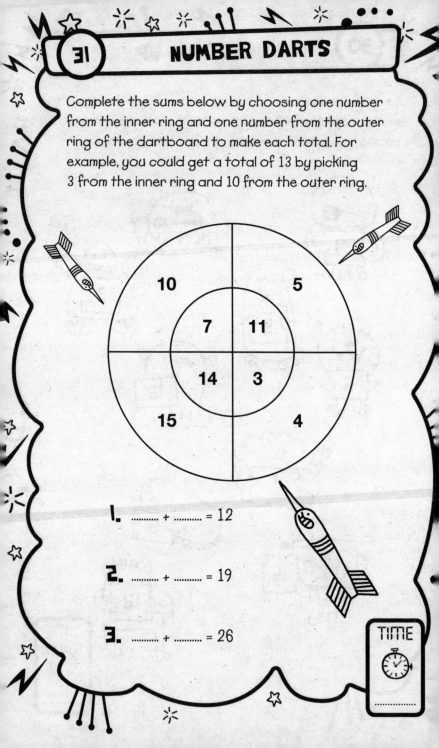

10   5

7   11

14   3

15   4

1. .... + ... = 12

2. .... + ... = 19

3. .... + ... = 26

TIME

....

CUBE CHALLENGE

In this example, eight blocks are arranged in a 2 x 2 x 2 cube.

EXAMPLE:

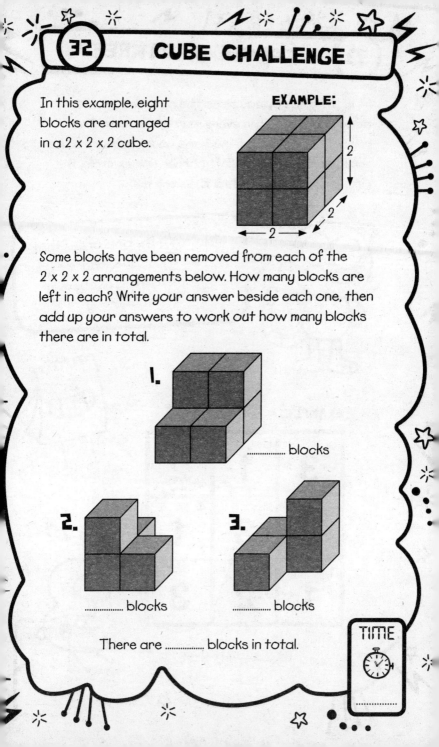

Some blocks have been removed from each of the 2 x 2 x 2 arrangements below. How many blocks are left in each? Write your answer beside each one, then add up your answers to work out how many blocks there are in total.

I.

.... blocks

2.

.... blocks

3.

.... blocks

There are .... blocks in total.

TIME

Fill in the grids opposite so the numbers 1 to 3 appear once each in every row and column. The numbers in each bold-lined area must add up to the small number in its top left corner. For example, the circled 1 and 3 add up to the small 4.

> Start with the bold areas that surround just one square – you can write these numbers in straight away.

EXAMPLE:

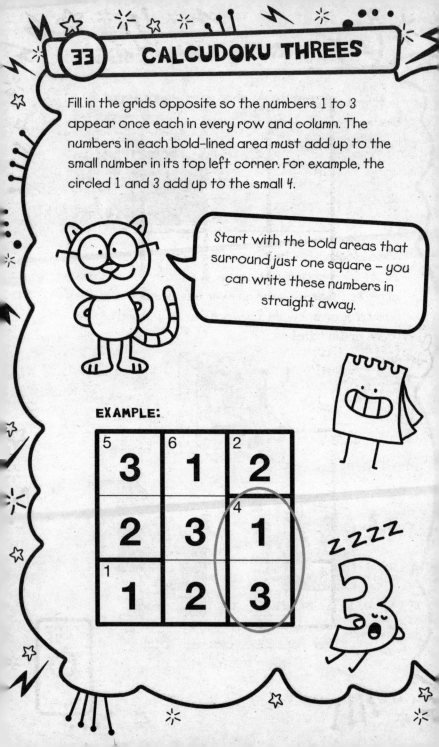

5 **3**	6 **1**	2 **2**
2	**3**	4 **1**
1 **1**	**2**	**3**

ZZZZ

1.

1	6	3
5		
		3

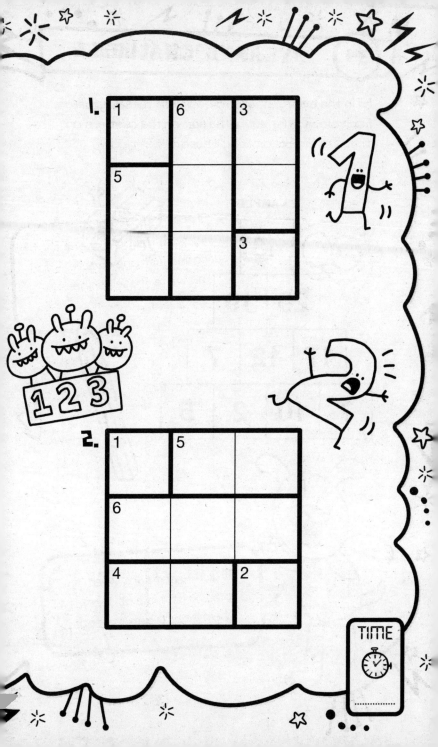

2.

1	5	
6		
4		2

TIME

....

34 PYRAMID CHALLENGE

Fill in the empty blocks to complete these pyramids. Each block must equal the sum of the numbers on the two blocks directly beneath it.

EXAMPLE:

| 48 |
29	19
17	12	7
7	10	2	5

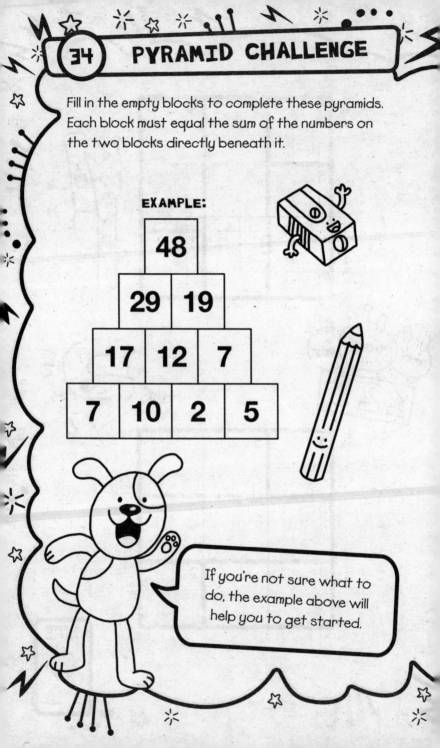

If you're not sure what to do, the example above will help you to get started.

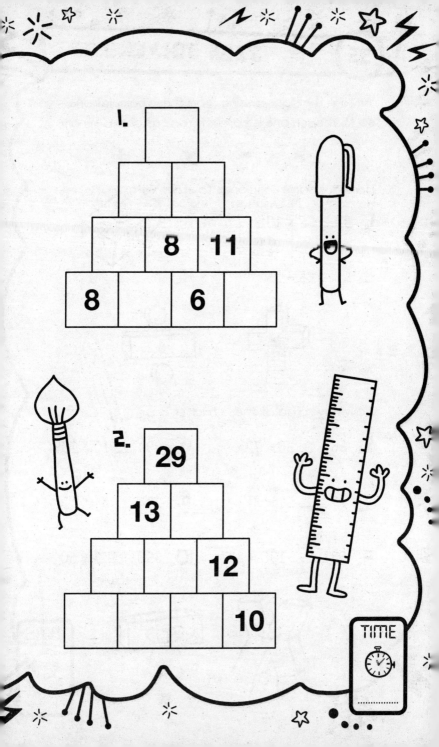

SIGN SOLVER

Write in the signs missing from these calculations so that each one is correct. You can choose from:

+   -   x   ÷

Here are some easy ones to start with:

1. 5 .... 5 = 10

2. 5 .... 5 = 1

3. 5 .... 5 = 25

4. 5 .... 5 = 0

Now have a go at these trickier ones:

5. 36 .... 36 = 72

6. 99 .... 10 = 109

7. 27 .... 54 = 81

8. 24 .... 8 = 3

9. 987 .... 100 = 887

10. 350 .... 7 = 50

TIME

PICTURE SUMS

The pig, sheep and hen shown below each represent a number. Can you use the picture sums to work out what they are? Fill in your answers at the bottom of the page.

= 7

= 10

= 9

= ....   = ...   = ...

TIME

....

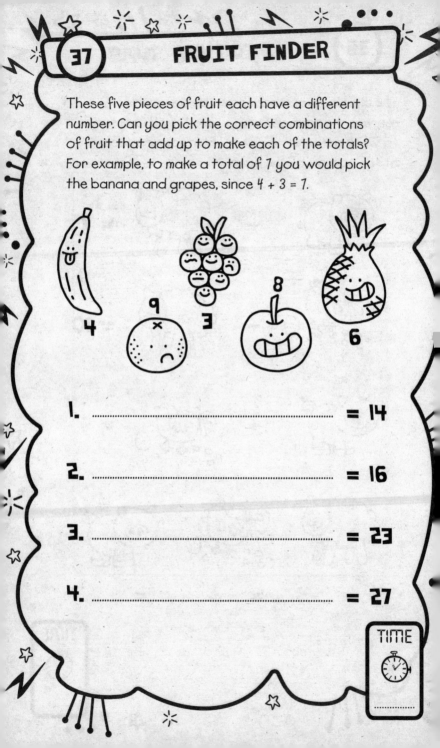

37 FRUIT FINDER

These five pieces of fruit each have a different number. Can you pick the correct combinations of fruit that add up to make each of the totals? For example, to make a total of 7 you would pick the banana and grapes, since 4 + 3 = 7.

4

9

3

8

6

1. .... = 14

2. .... = 16

3. .... = 23

4. .... = 27

TIME

ODD ONE OUT

Each of the monsters in this picture is holding a number. Can you work out which one is the odd one out and why?

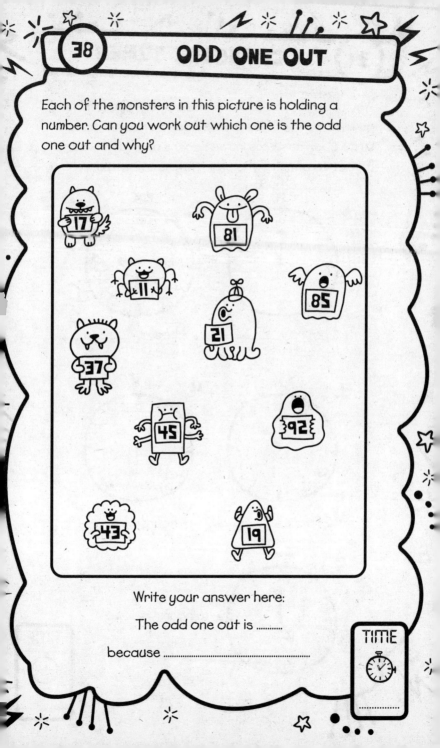

Write your answer here:

The odd one out is ....

because ....

TIME

....

CHANGING TIMES

What time would each of these clocks show if the given number of hours was added or subtracted? Write your answers in the spaces provided – don't forget to check if the start time is a.m. or p.m.

1. P.M.

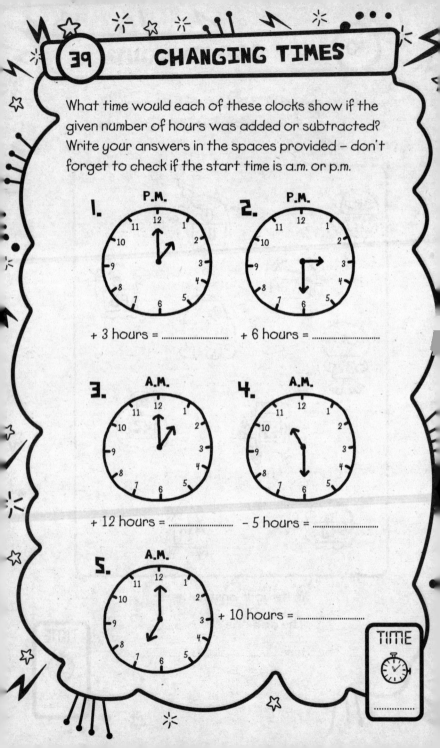

+ 3 hours = ...

2. P.M.

+ 6 hours = ...

3. A.M.

+ 12 hours = ...

4. A.M.

– 5 hours = ...

5. A.M.

+ 10 hours = ...

TIME

....

Complete these calculation chains by starting with the number on the left and performing each sum in turn to get the final result.

EXAMPLE:

10	+ 2	+ 5	– 12	=	_5_

1. 17   – 10   + 3   x 5   = ...

2. 25   ÷ 5   x 2   + 5   = ...

3. 50   – 10   ÷ 10   x 2   = ...

4. 9   + 2   x 5   + 101   = ...

TIME
....

NO PAIRS SQUARES

Complete this puzzle by writing a number from 1 to 6 in every empty square. No number can repeat within any row or column. No two touching squares – including diagonally touching squares – can contain the same number.

EXAMPLE:

1	2	5	3	4	6
3	6	4	2	5	1
2	5	1	6	3	4
6	4	3	5	1	2
5	1	2	4	6	3
4	3	6	1	2	5

	5			6	
		5	4		
		2	3		
	6			1	

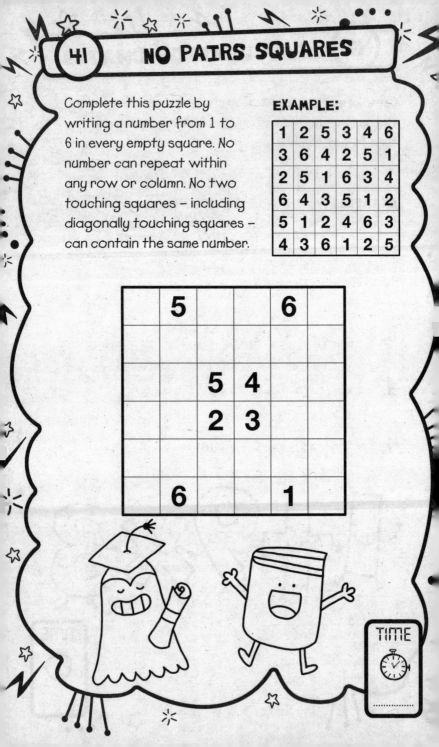

TIME

MONSTER MONEY

Far away in Monsterville, they have their own money system. It's made up of the following coins, known as 'mons' or 'm' for short.

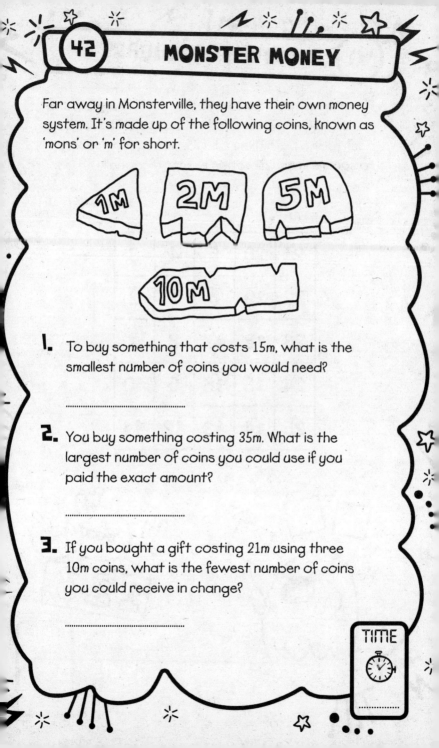

1. To buy something that costs 15m, what is the smallest number of coins you would need?

....

2. You buy something costing 35m. What is the largest number of coins you could use if you paid the exact amount?

....

3. If you bought a gift costing 21m using three 10m coins, what is the fewest number of coins you could receive in change?

....

TIME

....

PATH FINDERS

Place a number from 1 to 25 into each empty square, so no number repeats within the puzzle. The numbers must form a path from 1 to 25, moving from square to square in any direction except diagonally.

EXAMPLE:

21	20	5	4	3
22	19	6	7	2
23	18	17	8	1
24	15	16	9	10
25	14	13	12	11

1.

	24		4	
22	21		5	2
18	15		9	10
	16		12	

Chomp!

2.

		12		
	24	11	4	
		10		

TIME

Can you complete the brick wall by placing a number from 1 to 5 into each empty brick? Numbers cannot repeat in any row or column, and every bold-lined 2 x 1 brick must contain one even number and one odd number. Take a look at the example to see how it works.

EXAMPLE:

4	3	2	5	1
5	1	4	3	2
1	4	3	2	5
3	2	5	1	4
2	5	1	4	3

4	1			5
1				
		5		
				2
2			1	3

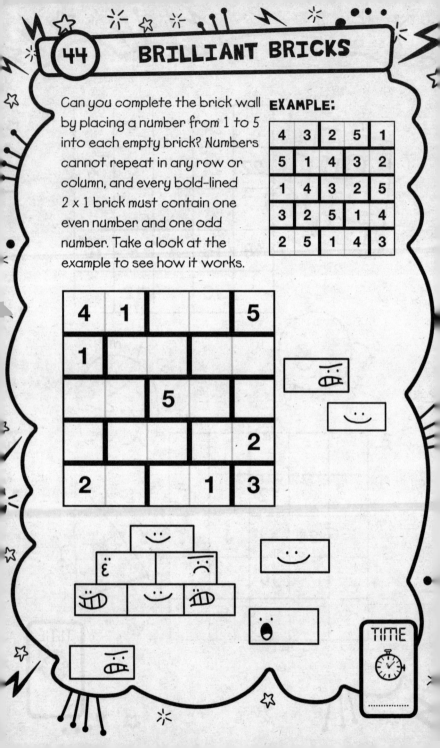

FIND THE SHAPE

Without actually trying it, imagine drawing straight lines to join the numbers below in each of the orders given underneath. What shape would you have drawn in each case? The example shows you how it works.

•1   •2   •3

•4   •5   •6

•7   •8   •9

EXAMPLE:
1 → 2 → 5 → 4 → 1 = square

1. 7 → 3 → 9 → 7 = ...

2. 8 → 2 → 3 → 9 → 8 = ...

3. 4 → 2 → 6 → 9 → 7 → 4 = ...

TIME

....

CUBE MAKER

Only one of these shapes can be folded along the black lines to make a complete, six-sided cube. Can you work out which one it is?

A.

B.

C.

D.

E.

TIME

TREASURE HUNT

Can you find the diamond rings hidden in each of these puzzles? The numbers tell you how many rings are in all the touching squares – including diagonally touching ones. The rings are only hidden in empty squares, and there can be no more than one ring per square. Happy hunting!

EXAMPLE:

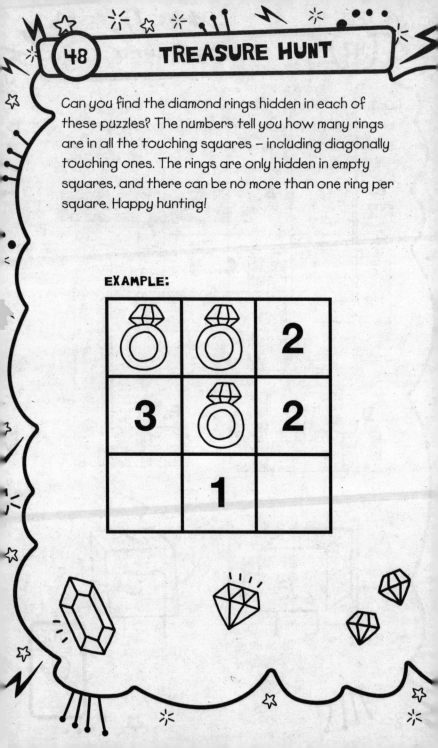

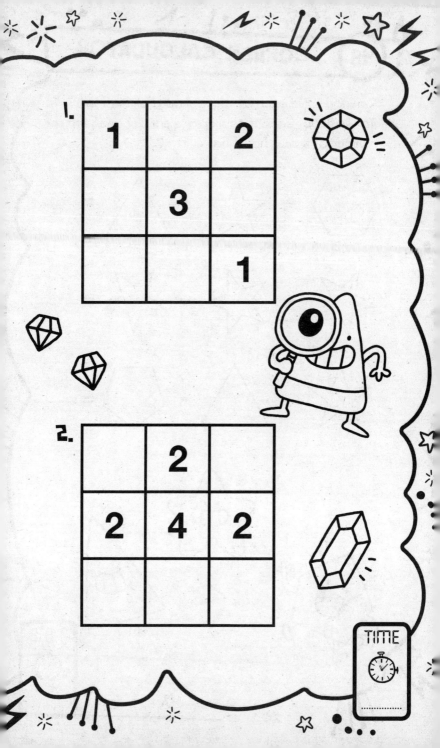

49 CORNER CALCULATOR

Can you solve each of these shape calculations?
To work out each total, replace each shape with the
number of sides that it has.

TIME

OCEAN FRIENDS

Each of these sea creatures has a number. Can you draw lines to sort them into pairs, so each sea creature is joined to another whose number is three times their value?

TIME

....

GREAT GRIDS

Fill in the grids so the numbers 1 to 3 appear once in every row and column. Here's the catch – numbers must be placed so that all of the 'greater than' signs (>) are correct.

> Greater than signs always point from the bigger to the smaller number of a pair. For example, you could have '2 > 1' since 2 is greater than 1, but '1 > 2' would be wrong because 1 is not greater than 2.

EXAMPLE:

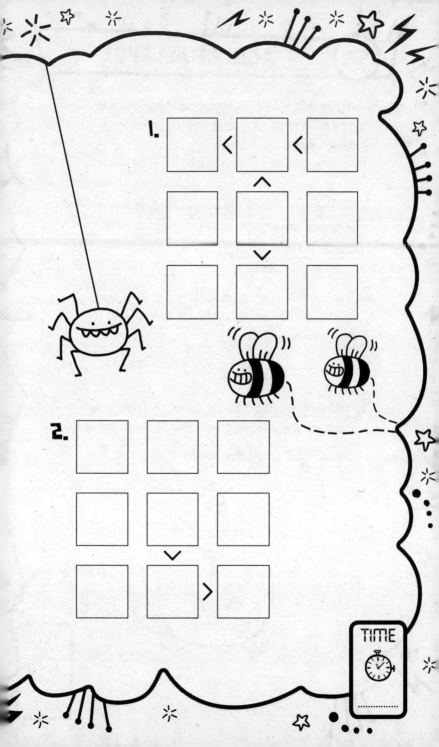

AGE CHALLENGE

Can you work out the ages of these people, based on the information given? Write your answers in the spaces below each question.

1. If Amira is 7 now, how old will she be in 5 years' time?

.... years old.

2. Lucas celebrated his 6th birthday in June last year. How old will he be by the time it is September next year?

.... years old.

3. If Jasmine will be twice as old in four years' time as she is now, then how old is she today?

.... years old.

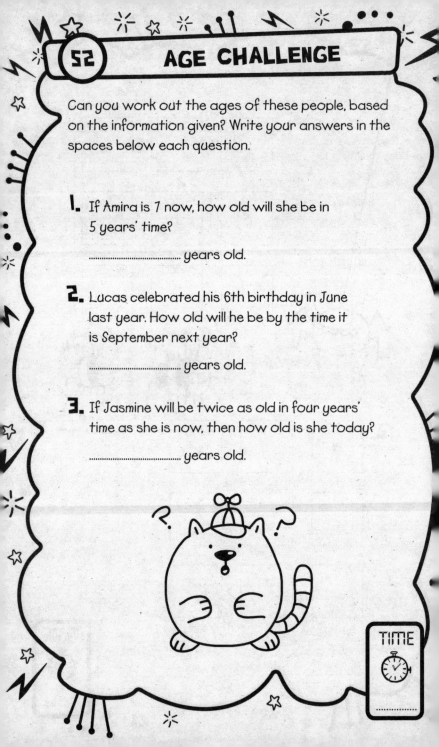

TIME

....

DO NOT TOUCH

Complete this puzzle by writing a number from 1 to 7 in every empty square, so no number repeats within any row or column. No two touching squares – including diagonally touching squares – can contain the same number.

EXAMPLE:

3	1	7	6	4	5	2
6	4	2	5	7	3	1
5	7	3	1	2	6	4
2	6	5	4	3	1	7
7	3	1	2	5	4	6
1	5	4	7	6	2	3
4	2	6	3	1	7	5

		3		6		
5	1				4	2
6	4				7	1
		6		5		

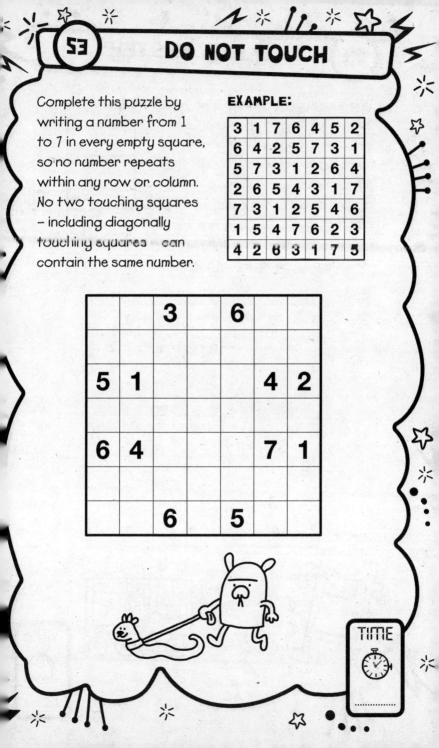

TIME

Draw along the dashed lines to divide the grid up into a set of rectangles, with one number per rectangle. Each number must end up inside a rectangle of that exact number of grid squares. For example, the 12 in the example is inside a 12-square rectangle.

EXAMPLE:

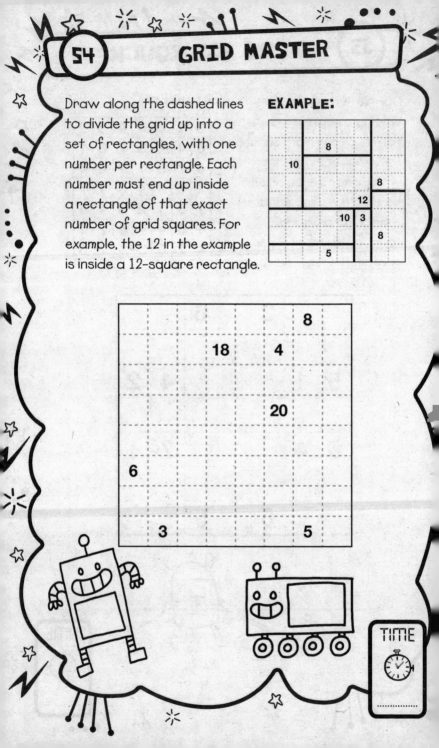

TIME

ALIEN SUPERMARKET

Find eight numbers from the three times table in this alien supermarket scene. Take care – other numbers not in the three times table are shown, too.

TIME

Fill in the empty blocks to complete these pyramids. Each block must equal the sum of the numbers on the two blocks directly beneath it.

EXAMPLE:

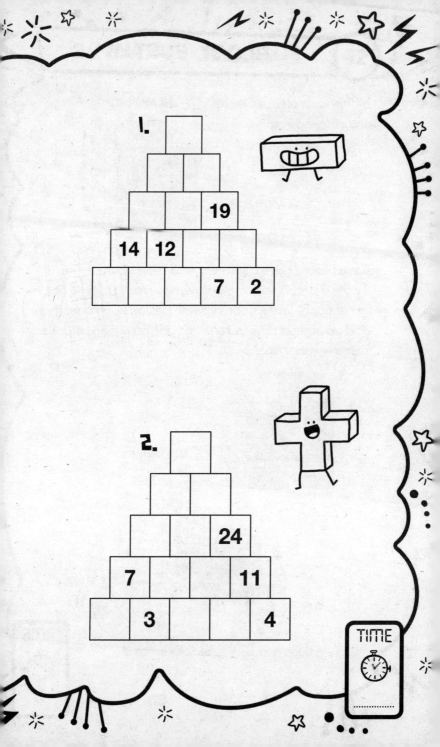

1.

		19

14	12		

			7	2

2.

		24

7			11

	3			4

TIME

BLOCK BUSTER

In this example, 18 blocks are stacked in a 3 x 2 x 3 arrangement.

EXAMPLE:

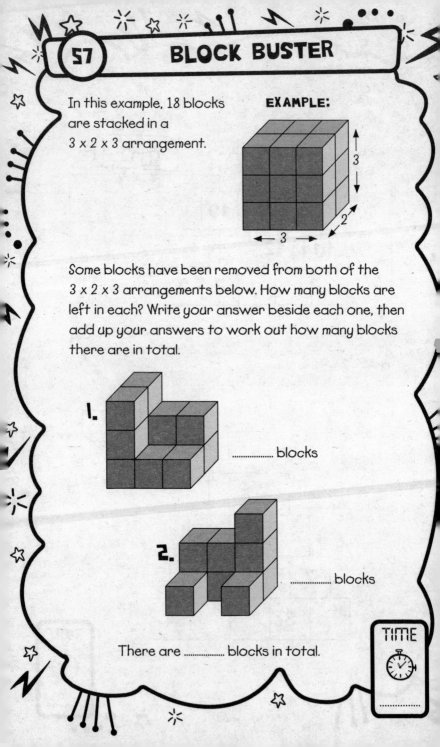

Some blocks have been removed from both of the 3 x 2 x 3 arrangements below. How many blocks are left in each? Write your answer beside each one, then add up your answers to work out how many blocks there are in total.

I.

.... blocks

2.

.... blocks

There are .... blocks in total.

TIME

....

OVERLAPPING SHAPES

The picture below has been made by drawing four overlapping polygons. Can you name them? Some types of shape may appear more than once.

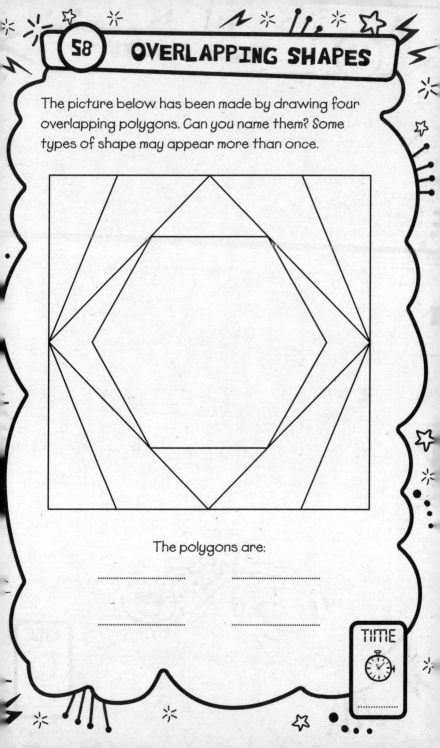

The polygons are:

....

....

TIME

....

BRAIN CHAINS

Complete these brain chains by starting with the number on the left and performing each sum in turn to get the final result.

EXAMPLE:

12   + 3   + 6   – 10   =   <u>11</u>

1. 25   – 8   + 10   – 15   = ...

2. 24   ÷ 2   × 3   – 6   = ...

3. 99   – 10   + 1   ÷ 10   × 3   = ...

4. 64   ÷ 8   × 5   – 7   + 66   = ...

TIME

....

A LONG TIME

Each of these entries shows two different amounts of time. Can you circle the time that is longest for each one?

1. 90 seconds   2 minutes

2. ½ a minute   45 seconds

3. 1 ½ hours   80 minutes

4. 3 weeks   20 days

5. 1 day   25 hours

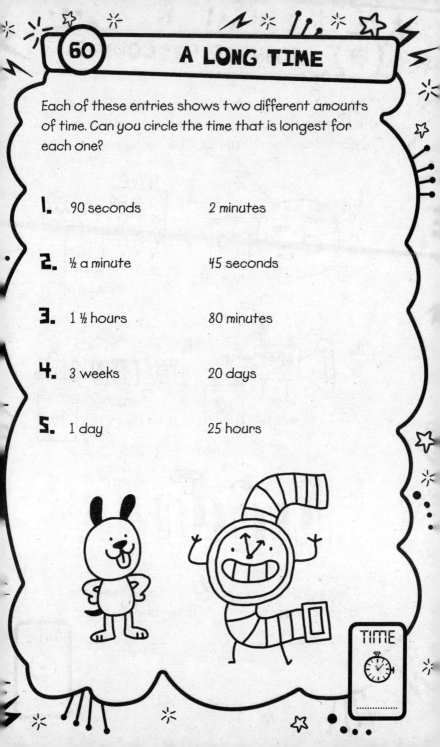

TIME

61 MONSTER DISCOUNTS

The monster music shop is having a big sale on all these instruments. Can you work out which is the cheapest and most expensive item after discount?

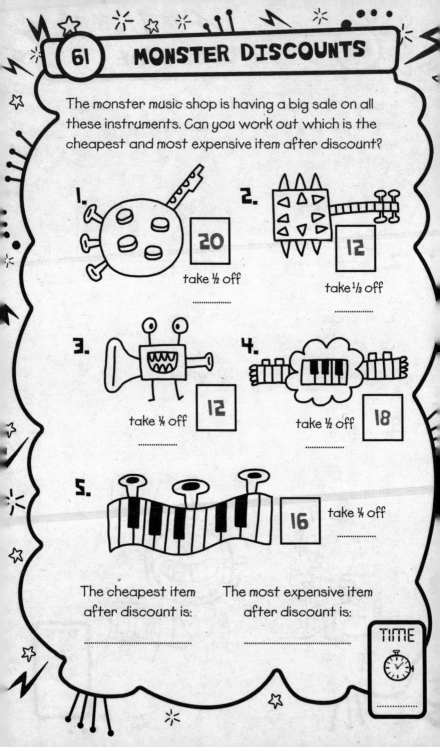

1. 20 take ½ off ....

2. 12 take ⅓ off ....

3. 12 take ¼ off ....

4. 18 take ½ off ....

5. 16 take ¼ off ....

The cheapest item after discount is:

....

The most expensive item after discount is:

....

TIME

....

THREE AWAY

Can you place the numbers 1 to 6 so they appear once each in every row and column? If two squares have a bar between them, the numbers must have a difference of 3. One pair of these numbers is circled in the example – notice how 4 – 1 = 3.

EXAMPLE:

6	1	5	3	2	4
4	3	2	5	1	6
5	2	6	1	4	3
3	4	1	2	6	5
1	5	4	6	3	2
2	6	3	4	5	1

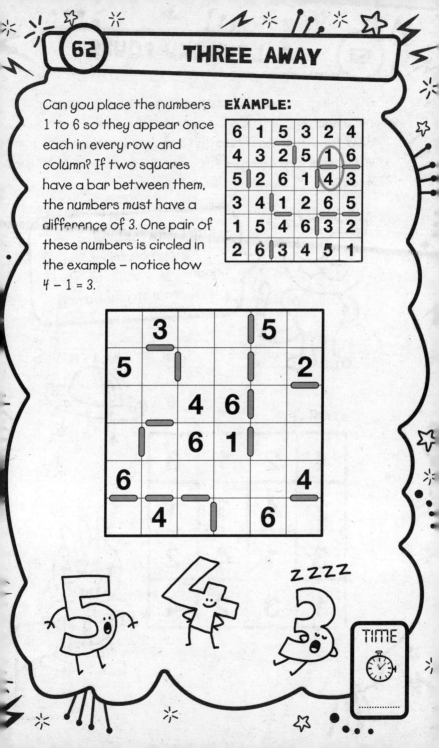

Fill in the grids opposite so the numbers 1 to 4 appear once each in every row and column. The numbers in each bold-lined area must add up to the small number in its top left corner. For example, the circled 4 and 2 add up to the small 6.

Start with the bold areas that surround just one square – you can write these numbers in straight away.

EXAMPLE:

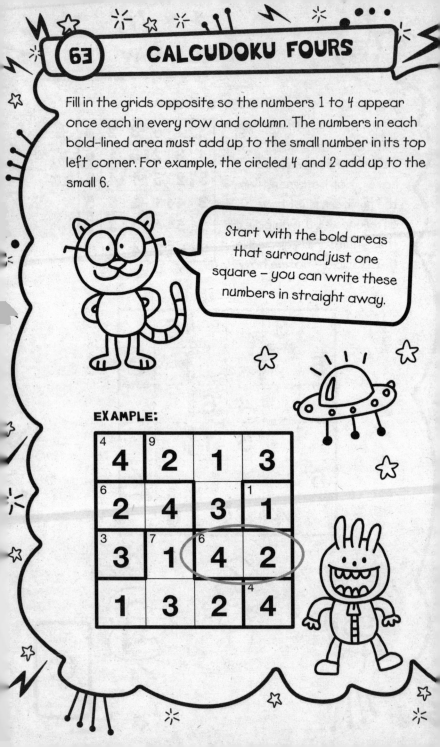

4 4	9 2	1	3
6 2	4	3	1 1
3 3	7 1	6 4	2
1	3	2	4 4

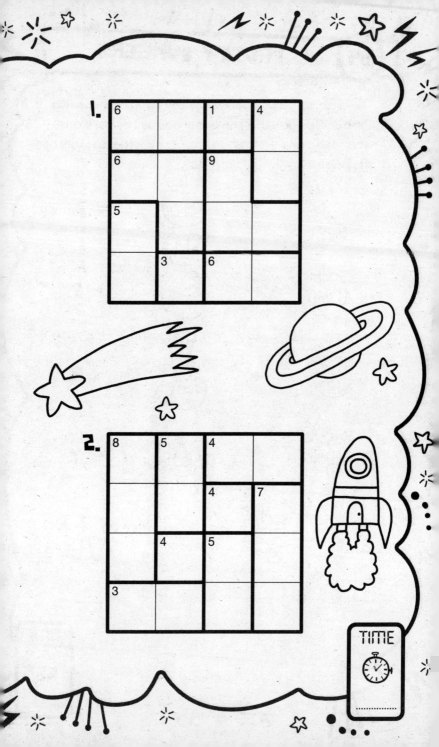

FRUITY NUMBERS

The different fruits shown below each represent a number. Can you use the picture sums to work out what they are? Fill in your answers at the bottom of the page.

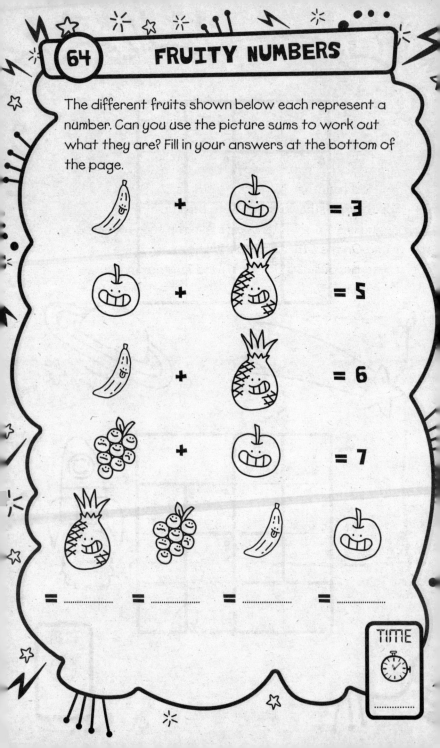

MYSTERY THREES

Look at the numbers on the board below. Can you circle the ones that are multiples of 3 and cross out the ones that are not multiples of 3?

If a number is a multiple of three, the individual digits will add together to make a multiple of three. For example, the number 567 is a multiple of 3, because 5 + 6 + 7 = 18, and 18 is in the three times table. On the other hand, 359 is not a multiple of three, because 3 + 5 + 9 = 17, and 17 is not in the three times table.

123   136   246

393   854   603

987   456   6879

ZZZZ

TIME

66 CUPCAKE CALCULATOR

Here are five numbered cupcakes. Choose cupcakes for each plate so that they add up to the number shown on it. You can use each cupcake once on each plate.

9 4 11 8

12 3

1. 14

2. 18

3. 25

4. 40

TIME

MONSTER JOURNEY

Help the monster to find the path through the maze to her truck. When you reach the car, go back to the start and add up just the numbers on the path. Then write your answer in the space below.

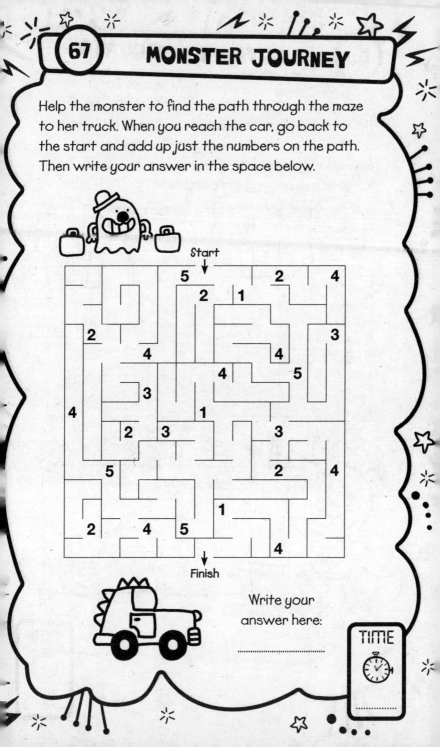

Start

5   2   4
2   1
2   3
4   4
4   5
3   1
4   2   3
3
2   3   3
5   2   4
1
2   4   5
4

Finish

Write your answer here:

....

TIME

RECTANGLE SPOTTER

It's time to test your shape-spotting skills. How many rectangles can you spot in the shape below? Look closely – the rectangles differ in size and some may overlap, too. Don't forget to include the large one all around the outside.

Write your answer here:

.... rectangles

TIME

....

NUMBER DARTS

Complete the sums below by choosing one number from the inner ring and one number from the outer ring of the dartboard to make each total. For example, you could make a total of 9 by picking 7 from the inner ring and 2 from the outer ring.

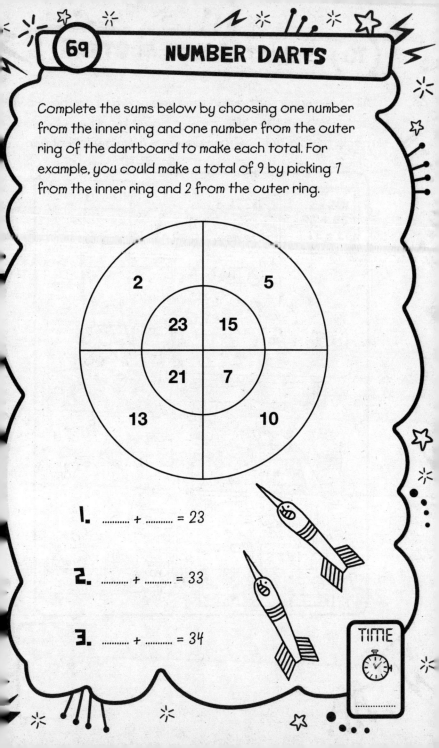

1. .... + ... = 23

2. .... + ... = 33

3. .... + ... = 34

TIME

....

MONSTER SUM SPOTTER

All of the sums that are in the same position on these two pictures have the same answer, apart from five. Can you circle the five sums whose answers have been changed?

Once you have found the five different sum results, can you also find five differences between the two pictures?

Fill in the grids so the numbers 1 to 4 appear once in every row and column. Here's the catch – numbers must be placed so that all of the 'greater than' signs (>) are correct.

Greater than signs always point from the bigger to the smaller number of a pair. For example, you could have '3 > 2' since 3 is greater than 2, but '2 > 3' would be wrong because 2 is not greater than 3.

EXAMPLE:

3 > 2   1   4

1   4   3   2

2 > 1   4 > 3

4 > 3   2   1

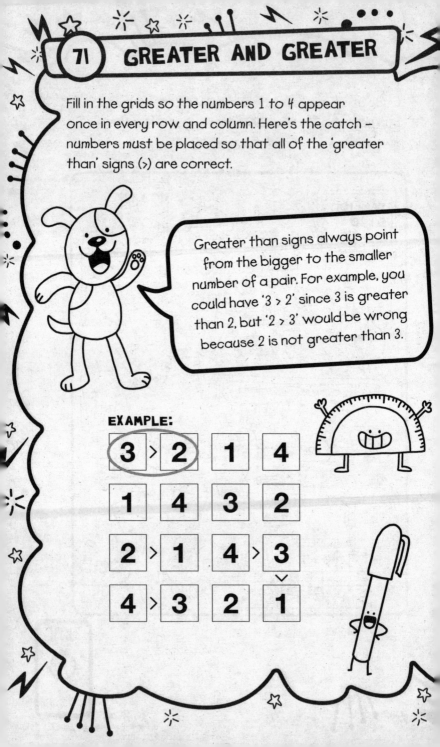

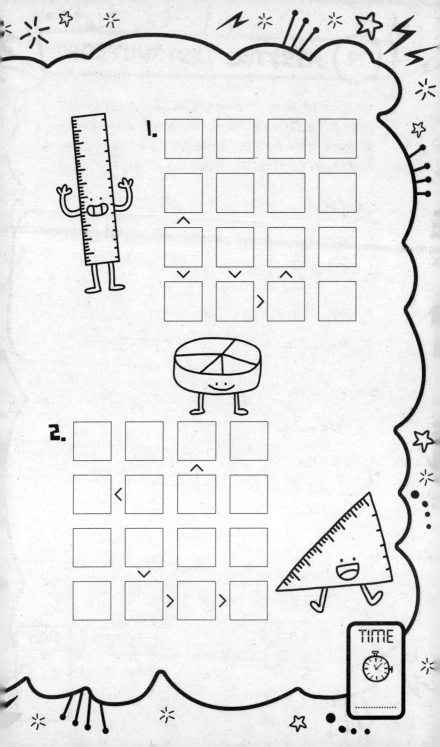

Each of the number rows below was created by applying a different rule to the starting number. In the example, the rule was + 2 since 1 + 2 = 3, then 3 + 2 = 5, and so on. Can you work out the four other rules?

EXAMPLE:

| 1 | 3 | 5 | 7 | 9 | 11 |

Rule: + 2

1. 99   87   75   63   51   39

Rule: ....

2. 5   11   17   23   29   35

Rule: ....

3. 34   30   26   22   18   14

Rule: ....

4. 2   4   8   16   32   64

Rule: ....

TIME

....

TRAIN YOUR BRAIN

Complete these brain chains by starting with the number on the left and performing each sum in turn to get the final result.

EXAMPLE:

45   + 5   ÷ 10   + 1   =   6

1. 85   – 15   – 25   + 10   = ...

2. 30   ÷ 3   x 4   + 5   – 6   = ...

3. 130   – 10   ÷ 10   x 4   + 10   + 2   = ...

4. 170   – 20   ÷ 5   + 7   – 12   + 3   = ...

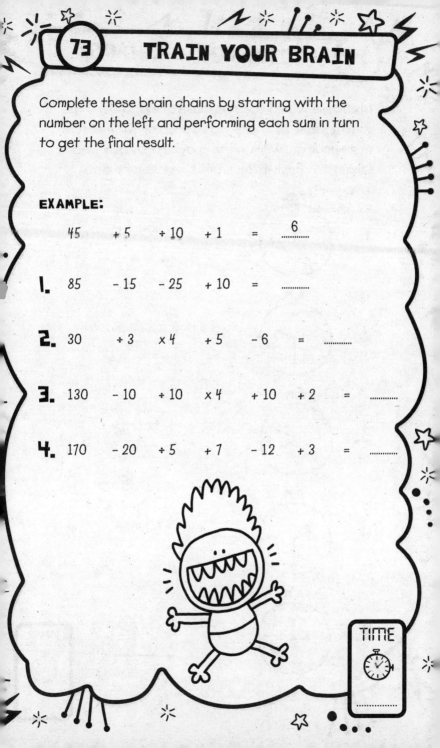

TIME

TIME FOR A CHANGE

What time would each of these clocks show if the given number of hours was added or subtracted? Write your answers in the spaces provided – don't forget to check if the start time is a.m. or p.m.

1. P.M.

+ 4 hours =

....

2. A.M.

+ 8 hours 30 minutes =

....

3. A.M.

– 11 hours =

....

4. P.M.

+ 7 hours =

....

5. A.M.

+ 3 hours 30 minutes =

....

TIME

....

MONEY MATTERS

On planet Zork, they have their own money system made up of the following coins, known as 'zorkies', or 'z' for short.

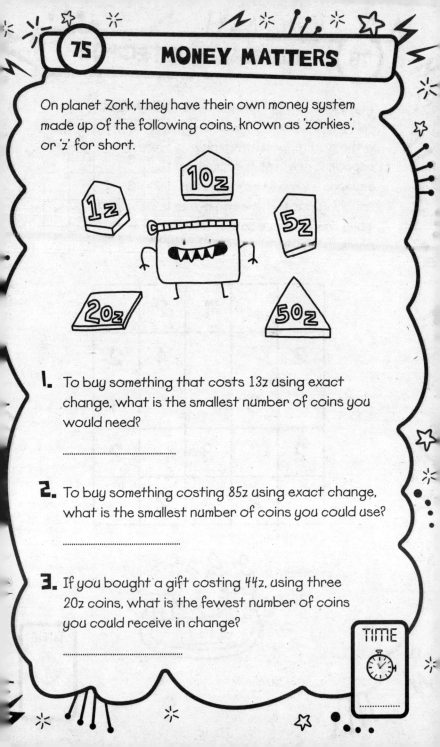

1. To buy something that costs 13z using exact change, what is the smallest number of coins you would need?

....

2. To buy something costing 85z using exact change, what is the smallest number of coins you could use?

....

3. If you bought a gift costing 44z, using three 20z coins, what is the fewest number of coins you could receive in change?

....

TIME

....

Can you find all of the cupcakes in the grid below? The numbers in the grid tell you how many cupcakes are in all the touching squares – including diagonally touching ones. There can be no more than one cupcake in any one square.

EXAMPLE:

	3		3	
	3			2
2	3	2		
	3		2	1
		2		1

		1	2	
2			4	2
	3			1
2		3		2
	2		2	

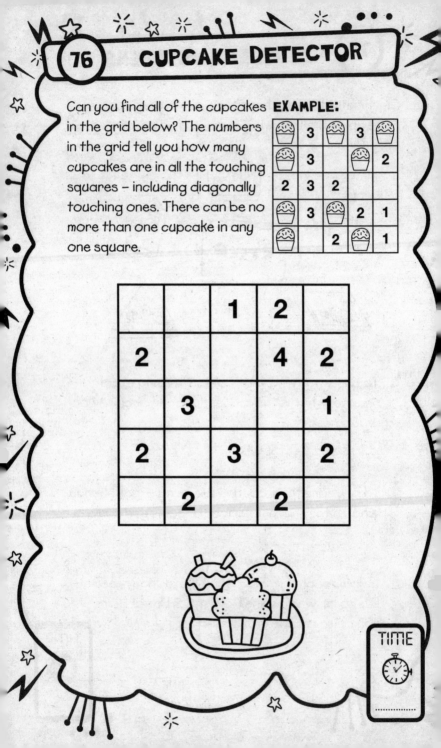

TIME

SEQUENCE SUPERHERO

Can you work out which number comes next in each of the following mathematical sequences?

EXAMPLE:

| 98 | 92 | 86 | 80 | 74 | 68 | _62_ |

1. 33   36   39   42   45   48   ....

2. 150   142   134   126   118   110   ....

3. 13   22   31   40   49   58   ....

4. 64   32   16   8   4   2   ....

TIME

....

SUDOKU MASTER

Use your skills to fill in the sudoku puzzles opposite. Place the numbers 1 to 4 so they appear once each in every row, column and bold-lined 2 x 2 area. The numbers outside the grid are the sum of the nearest two numbers in that row or column.

In the circled area, notice how the 6 clue is solved by the 4 and 2, since 6 = 4 + 2.

EXAMPLE:

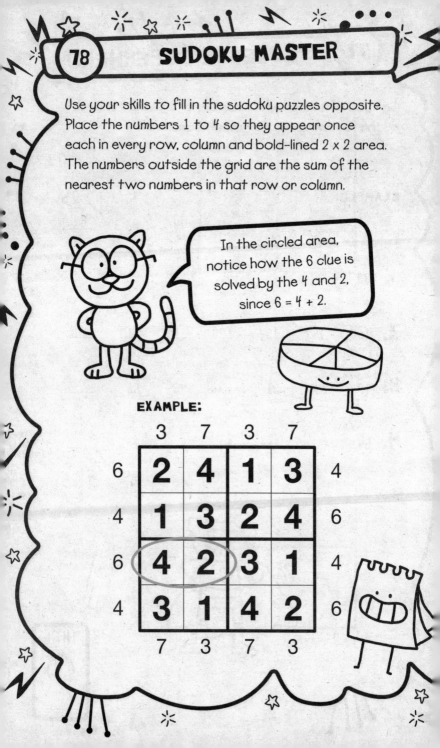

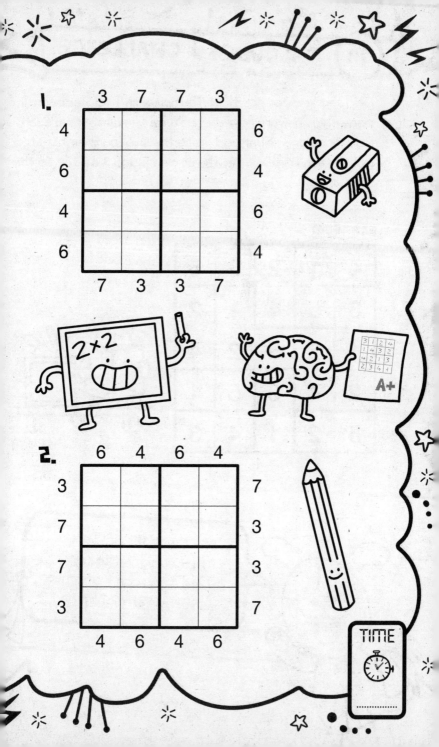

1.

	3	7	7	3	
4					6
6					4
4					6
6					4
	7	3	3	7	

2.

	6	4	6	4	
3					7
7					3
7					3
3					7
	4	6	4	6	

Fill in the grids opposite so the numbers 1 to 5 appear once each in every row and column. The numbers in each bold-lined area must add up to the small number in its top left corner. For example, the circled 5 and 3 add up to the small 8.

EXAMPLE:

5		6	8	
4	1	2	3	5
3	5		15	6
3	5	4	1	2
3				
1	3	5	2	4
		4	5	1
2	4	3	5	1
7			7	
5	2	1	4	3

Start with the bold areas that surround just one square – you can write these numbers in straight away.

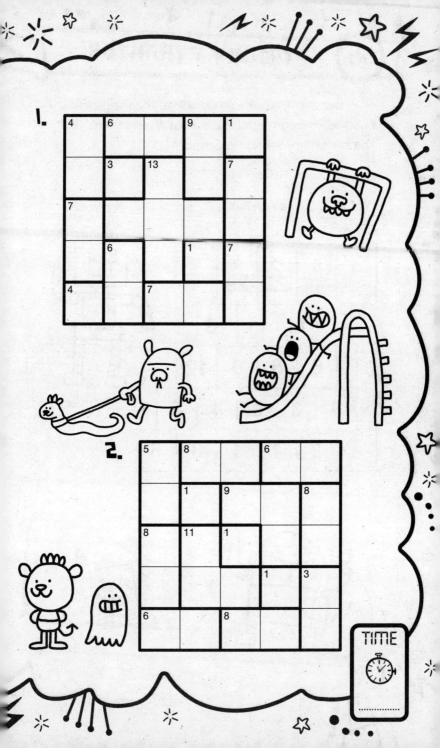

1.

4	6		9	1
	3	13		7
7				
	6		1	7
4		7		

2.

5	8		6	
	1	9		8
8	11	1		
			1	3
6		8		

TIME

....

TRICKY PYRAMIDS

Fill in the empty blocks to complete these pyramids. Each block must equal the sum of the numbers on the two blocks directly beneath it.

EXAMPLE:

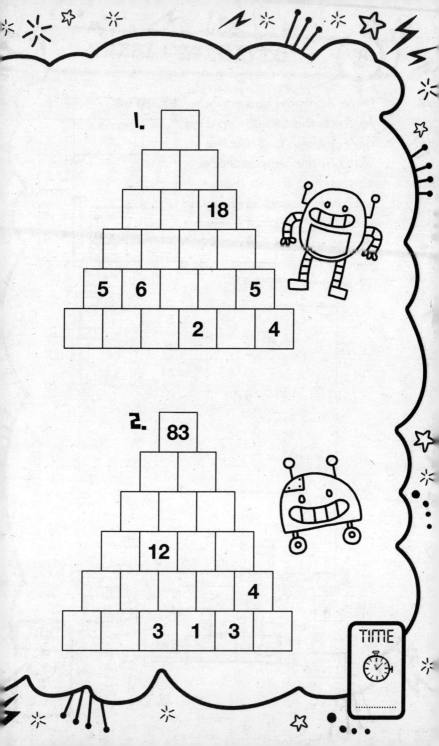

DIVIDING LINES

Draw along the dashed lines to divide the grid up into a set of rectangles *and* squares, with one number per shape. You must do this so that each number ends up inside a shape of that exact number of grid squares. For example, the 12 in the example is inside a 12-square rectangle.

EXAMPLE:

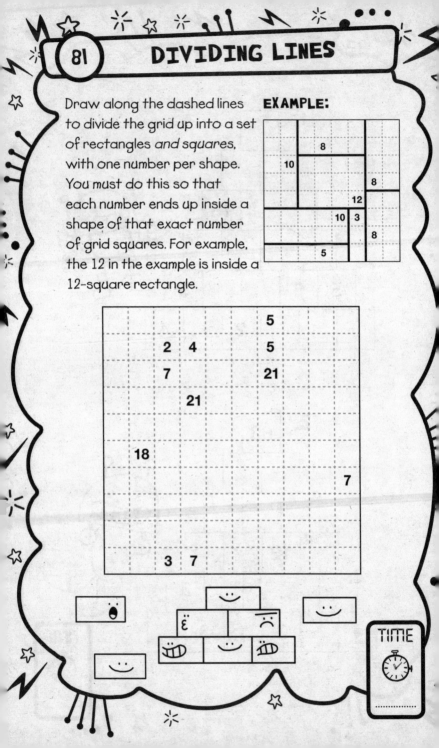

NUMBER TARGET

Complete the sums below by choosing one number from each ring of the dartboard to make each total given. For example, you could make a total of 7 by picking 4 from the inner ring, 2 from the middle ring and 1 from the outer ring.

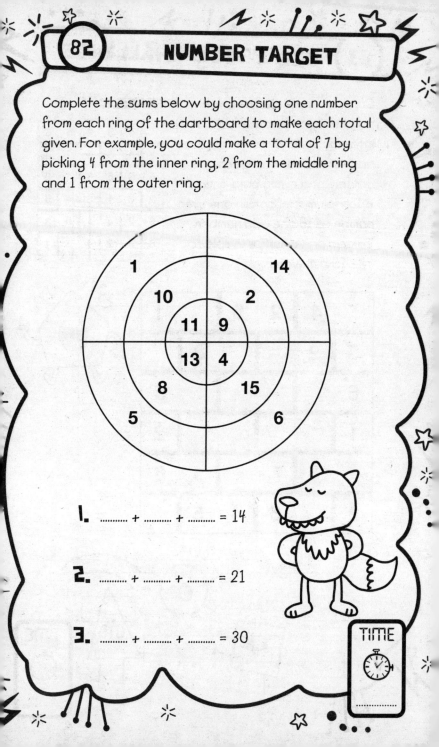

1   14

10   2

11 | 9

13 | 4

8   15

5   6

1. .... + ... + ... = 14

2. .... + ... + ... = 21

3. .... + ... + ... = 30

TIME

....

Can you complete the brick wall by placing a number from 1 to 6 into each empty brick? Numbers cannot repeat in any row or column, and every bold-lined 2 x 1 brick must contain one even number and one odd number. Take a look at the example to see how it works.

EXAMPLE:

1	4	3	2	5	6
3	1	6	5	2	4
4	3	5	6	1	2
2	6	1	3	4	5
5	2	4	1	6	3
6	5	2	4	3	1

	4	2	5		1
5	2			3	
6					5
1					2
	5			1	6
2		6	4	5	

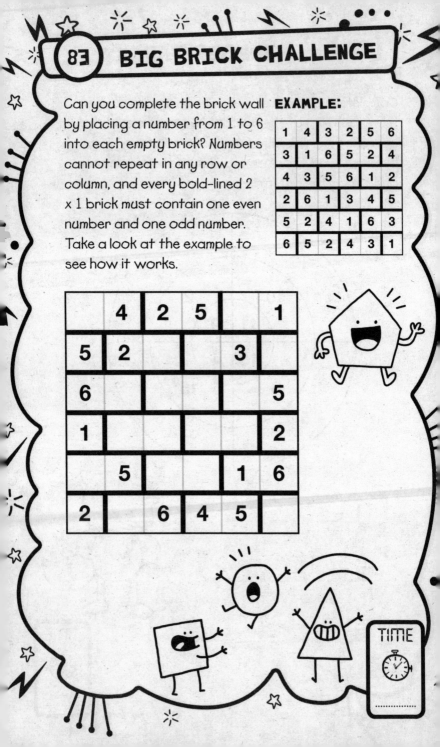

ALL THE ANSWERS

ANSWERS

MATHS GAME 1

The robot buddies are:

2 and 4
5 and 10
7 and 14
9 and 18

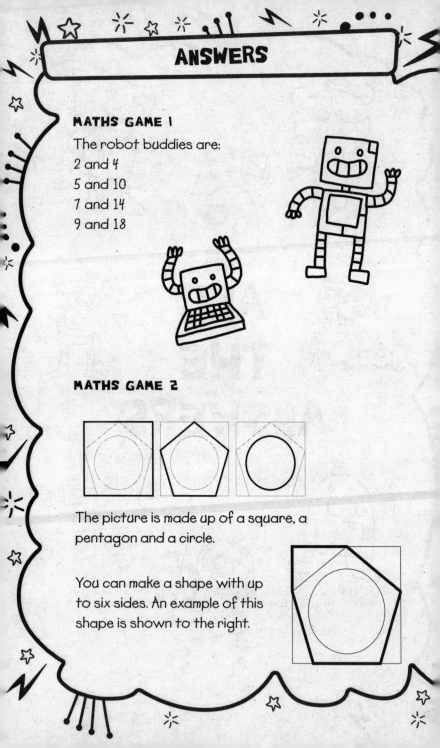

MATHS GAME 2

The picture is made up of a square, a pentagon and a circle.

You can make a shape with up to six sides. An example of this shape is shown to the right.

MATHS GAME 3

The odd numbers are:
3, 9, 13, 21, 37, 45, 67, 81, 101 and 135.

MATHS GAME 4

1. 11 = 4 + 7

2. 14 = 4 + 10

3. 16 = 4 + 5 + 7

4. 25 = 7 + 8 + 10

MATHS GAME 5

 = 3

 = 5

MATHS GAME 6

Start

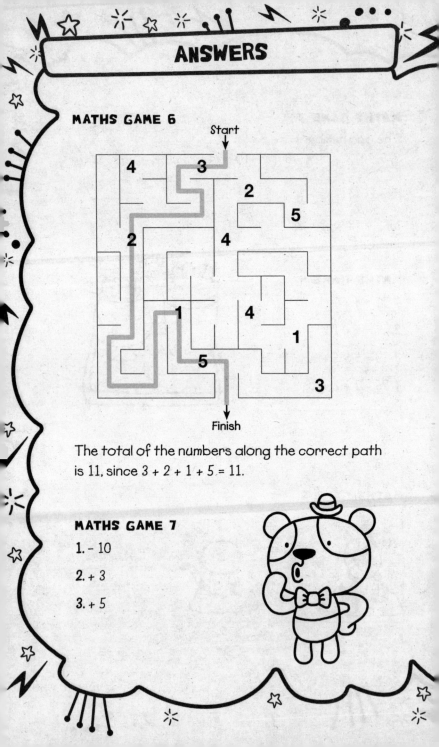

Finish

The total of the numbers along the correct path is 11, since 3 + 2 + 1 + 5 = 11.

MATHS GAME 7

1. – 10

2. + 3

3. + 5

MATHS GAME 8

1. $3 \times 5 = 15$ 2. $5 \times 5 = 25$

3. $4 + 8 = 12$ 4. $20 \div 2 = 10$

5. $19 + 19 = 38$ 6. $35 \div 5 = 7$

7. $87 + 13 = 100$ 8. $99 - 12 = 87$

9. $5 - 5 = 0$ 10. $11 \times 10 = 110$

MATHS GAME 9

3	4	2	1	5	6
4	5	3	6	2	1
6	1	4	2	3	5
1	2	5	4	6	3
2	3	6	5	1	4
5	6	1	3	4	2

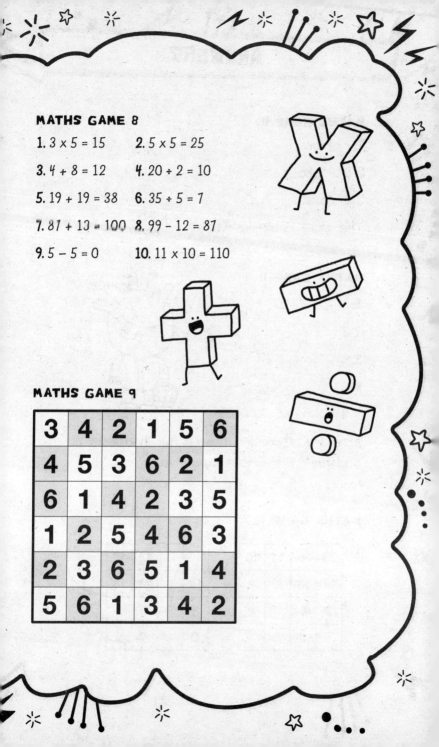

ANSWERS

MATHS GAME 10

1. 7 blocks

2. 5 blocks

3. 3 blocks

There are 15 blocks in total.

MATHS GAME 11

1. 3

2. 3

3. 4

4. 2

5. 6

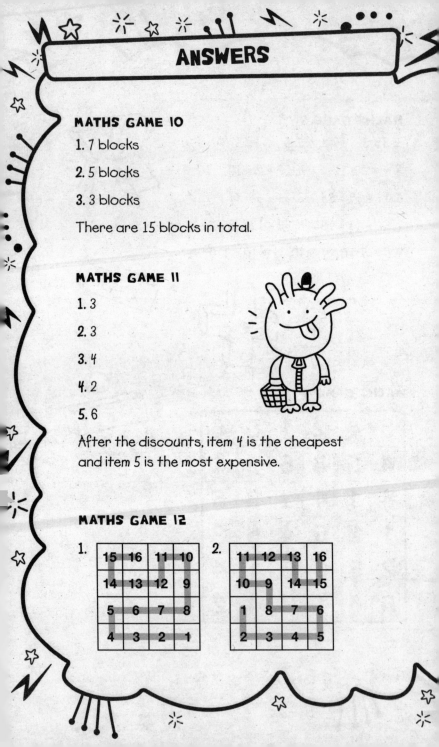

After the discounts, item 4 is the cheapest and item 5 is the most expensive.

MATHS GAME 12

1.

15	16	11	10
14	13	12	9
5	6	7	8
4	3	2	1

2.

11	12	13	16
10	9	14	15
1	8	7	6
2	3	4	5

MATHS GAME 13

1. 4 + 3 (= 7) changed to 3 + 5 (= 8)

2. 8 + 2 (= 10) changed to 1 + 8 (= 9)

3. 9 x 5 (= 45) changed to 40 + 4 (= 44)

4. 22 + 11 (= 33) changed to 10 + 20 (= 30)

5. 80 + 10 (= 90) changed to 8 x 10 (= 80)

The locations of the changed sums are numbered in the picture below. The five differences to the picture are also circled below.

ANSWERS

MATHS GAME 14

1.

	7	3	3	7	
4	3	1	2	4	6
6	4	2	1	3	4
4	1	3	4	2	6
6	2	4	3	1	4
	3	7	7	3	

2.

	6	4	4	6	
3	2	1	3	4	7
7	4	3	1	2	3
3	1	2	4	3	7
7	3	4	2	1	3
	4	6	6	4	

MATHS GAME 15

4	3	5	2	1
5	4	1	3	2
2	1	3	4	5
3	5	2	1	4
1	2	4	5	3

MATHS GAME 16

3	2	4	1
4	1	3	2
2	4	1	3
1	3	2	4

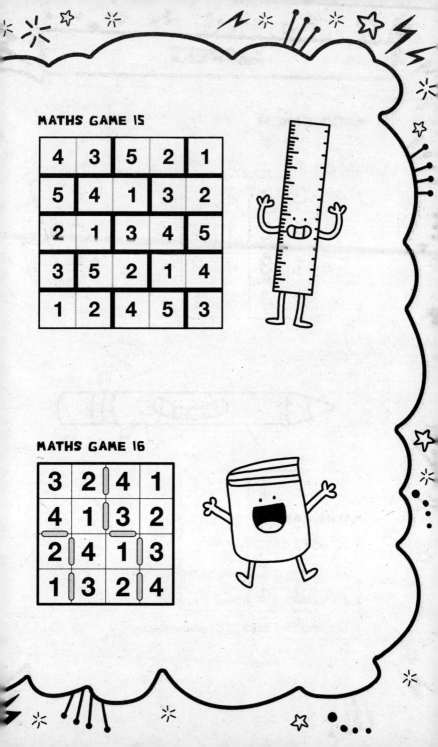

ANSWERS

MATHS GAME 17

E	G	F	A
fifteen	seventy	thirty	two
2	6	7	8

C	B	H	D
nine	five	eighty	fourteen
5	3	1	4

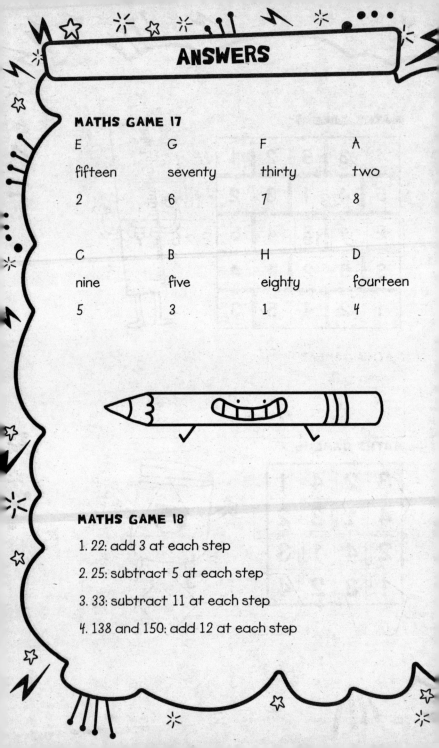

MATHS GAME 18

1. 22: add 3 at each step
2. 25: subtract 5 at each step
3. 33: subtract 11 at each step
4. 138 and 150: add 12 at each step

MATHS GAME 19

1.

```
        38
     15    23
    7    8    15
```

2.

```
        31
     18    13
    12    6    7
```

MATHS GAME 20

□ + △ + △ = 10

⬡ + ▯ + △ = 13

⬠ + ⬡ + ◇ = 15

ANSWERS

MATHS GAME 21

3	2	6	5	4	1
4	5	1	2	3	6
1	3	4	6	5	2
2	6	5	3	1	4
5	1	2	4	6	3
6	4	3	1	2	5

MATHS GAME 22

1.
2 < 3 > 1
∧   ∨   ∧
3 > 1 < 2
∨   ∧   ∧
1 < 2 < 3

2.
1 < 3 > 2
∧   ∨   ∨
3 > 2 > 1
∨   ∨   ∧
2 > 1 < 3

MATHS GAME 23

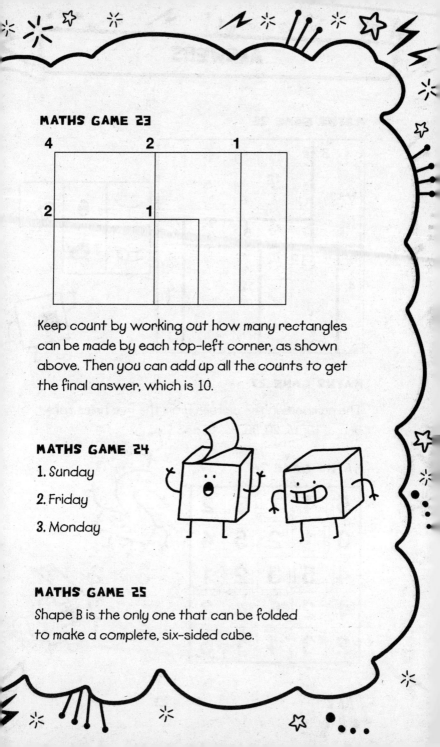

4		2		1

| 2 | | 1 | | |

Keep count by working out how many rectangles can be made by each top-left corner, as shown above. Then you can add up all the counts to get the final answer, which is 10.

MATHS GAME 24

1. Sunday

2. Friday

3. Monday

MATHS GAME 25

Shape B is the only one that can be folded to make a complete, six-sided cube.

ANSWERS

MATHS GAME 26

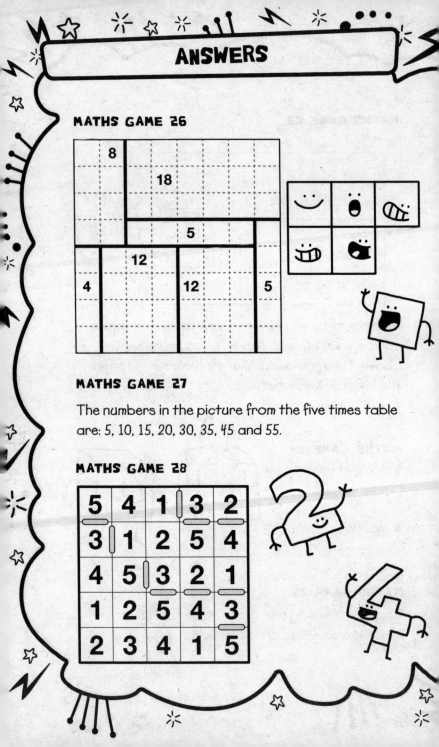

MATHS GAME 27

The numbers in the picture from the five times table are: 5, 10, 15, 20, 30, 35, 45 and 55.

MATHS GAME 28

5	4	1	3	2
3	1	2	5	4
4	5	3	2	1
1	2	5	4	3
2	3	4	1	5

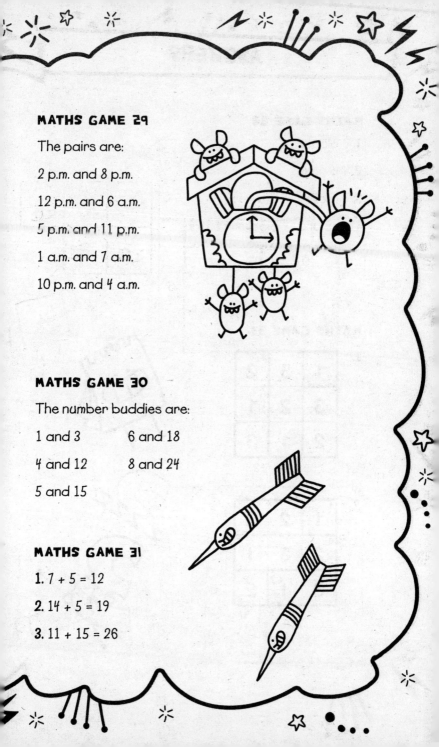

MATHS GAME 29

The pairs are:

2 p.m. and 8 p.m.

12 p.m. and 6 a.m.

5 p.m. and 11 p.m.

1 a.m. and 7 a.m.

10 p.m. and 4 a.m.

MATHS GAME 30

The number buddies are:

1 and 3   6 and 18

4 and 12   8 and 24

5 and 15

MATHS GAME 31

1. 7 + 5 = 12

2. 14 + 5 = 19

3. 11 + 15 = 26

ANSWERS

MATHS GAME 32

1. 6 blocks

2. 4 blocks

3. 4 blocks

There are 14 blocks in total.

MATHS GAME 33

1.

¹1	⁶3	³2
⁵3	2	1
2	1	³3

2.

¹1	⁵2	3
⁶2	3	1
⁴3	1	²2

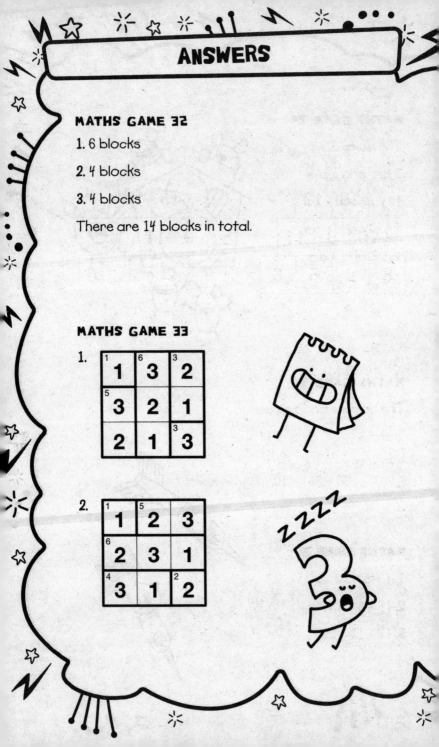

MATHS GAME 34

1.

		37		
	18	19	
10	8	11
8	2	6	5

2.

		29		
	13	16	
9	4	12
7	2	2	10

MATHS GAME 35

1. $5 + 5 = 10$ **2.** $5 + 5 = 1$

3. $5 \times 5 = 25$ **4.** $5 - 5 = 0$

5. $36 + 36 = 72$ **6.** $99 + 10 = 109$

7. $27 + 54 = 81$ **8.** $24 \div 8 = 3$

9. $987 - 100 = 887$ **10.** $350 \div 7 = 50$

MATHS GAME 36

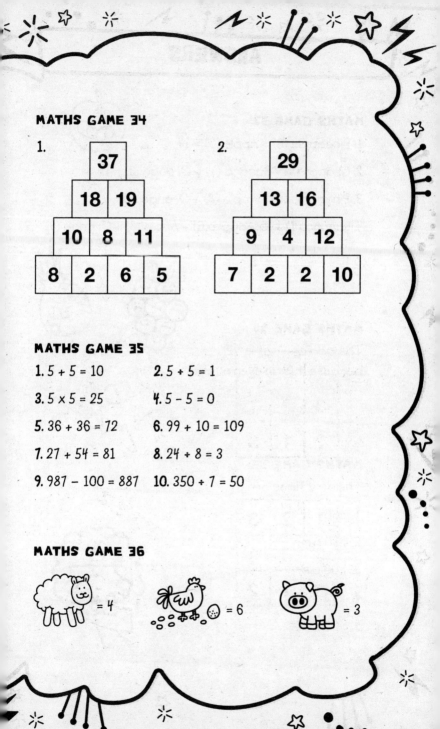

ANSWERS

MATHS GAME 37

1. Pineapple (6) + Apple (8) = 14

2. Grapes (3) + Banana (4) + Orange (9) = 16

3. Pineapple (6) + Apple (8) + Orange (9) = 23

4. Banana (4) + Pineapple (6) + Apple (8) + Orange (9) = 27

MATHS GAME 38

The odd one out is 92,
because it is an even number.

MATHS GAME 39

The new times are:

1. 4:00 p.m.

2. 9:30 p.m.

3. 1:00 p.m.

4. 6:30 a.m.

5. 5:00 p.m.

MATHS GAME 40

1. 50

2. 15

3. 8

4. 156

$1 + 9 \times 3$

MATHS GAME 41

1	5	3	2	6	4
4	2	6	1	3	5
3	1	5	4	2	6
6	4	2	3	5	1
5	3	1	6	4	2
2	6	4	5	1	3

ANSWERS

MATHS GAME 42

1. 2 coins: 10m + 5m (if using exact change) or 10m + 10m (if we were expecting change back)

2. 35 coins: 35 x 1m

3. If you paid 30m you would receive 9m back.
The smallest number is 3 coins: 5m + 2m + 2m.

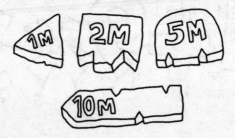

MATHS GAME 43

1.

23	24	25	4	3
22	21	6	5	2
19	20	7	8	1
18	15	14	9	10
17	16	13	12	11

2.

17	16	15	14	1
18	25	12	13	2
19	24	11	4	3
20	23	10	5	6
21	22	9	8	7

MATHS GAME 44

4	1	3	2	5
1	3	2	5	4
3	2	5	4	1
5	4	1	3	2
2	5	4	1	3

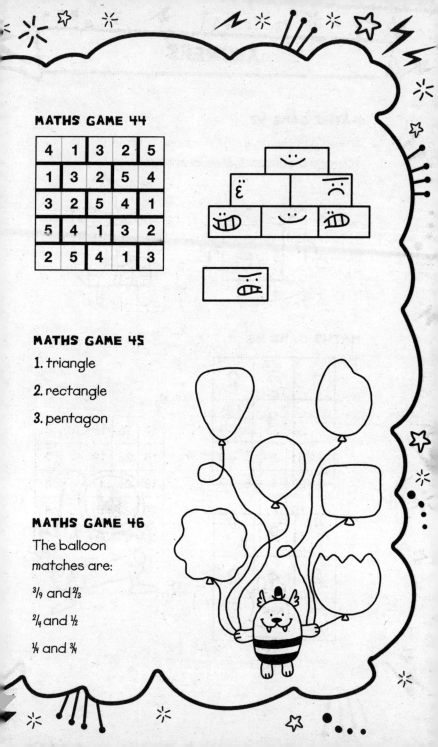

MATHS GAME 45

1. triangle

2. rectangle

3. pentagon

MATHS GAME 46

The balloon
matches are:

$^3/_9$ and $^2/_3$

$^2/_4$ and $^1/_2$

$^1/_4$ and $^3/_4$

MATHS GAME 47

Shape C is the only one that can be folded to make a complete, six-sided cube.

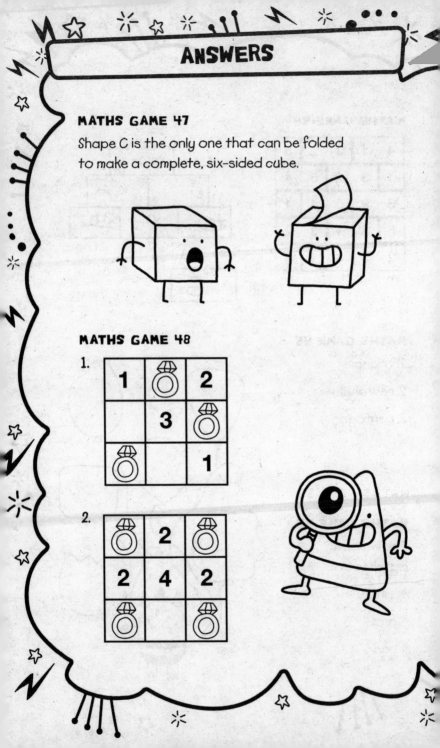

MATHS GAME 48

1.

1	💍	2
	3	💍
💍		1

2.

💍	2	💍
2	4	2
💍		💍

MATHS GAME 49

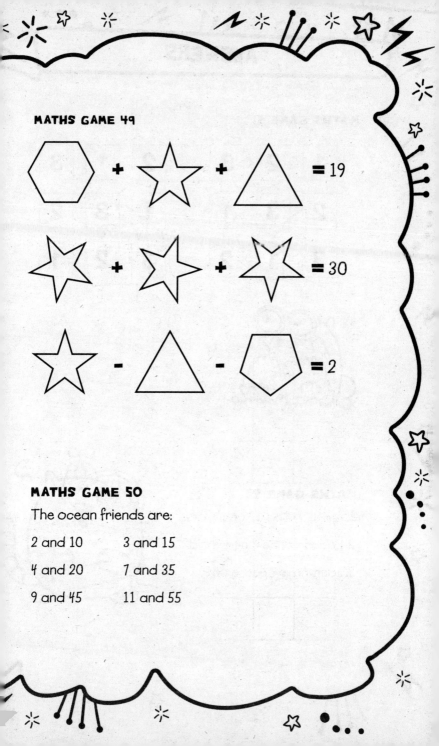

hexagon + star + triangle = 19

star + star + star = 30

star − triangle − pentagon = 2

MATHS GAME 50

The ocean friends are:

2 and 10   3 and 15

4 and 20   7 and 35

9 and 45   11 and 55

ANSWERS

MATHS GAME 51

1.

1 <	2 <	3
2	3 ^	1
3	1 ∨	2

2.

2	1	3
1	3	2
3	2 ∨ >	1

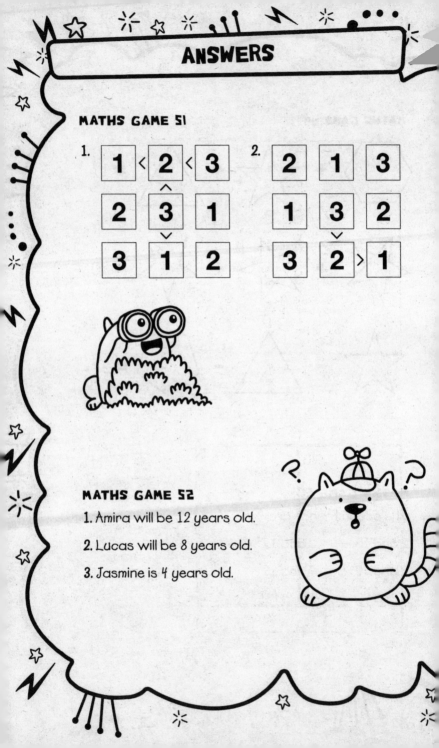

MATHS GAME 52

1. Amira will be 12 years old.

2. Lucas will be 8 years old.

3. Jasmine is 4 years old.

MATHS GAME 53

4	5	3	1	6	2	7
2	6	4	5	7	1	3
5	1	7	6	3	4	2
7	3	2	4	1	5	6
6	4	5	3	2	7	1
3	2	1	7	4	6	5
1	7	6	2	5	3	4

MATHS GAME 54

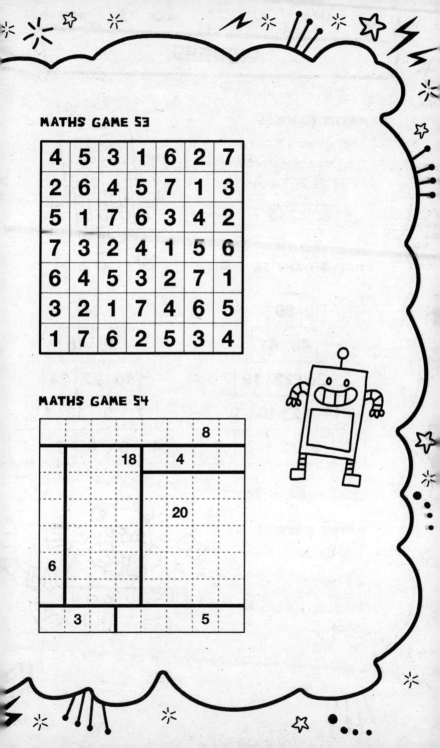

ANSWERS

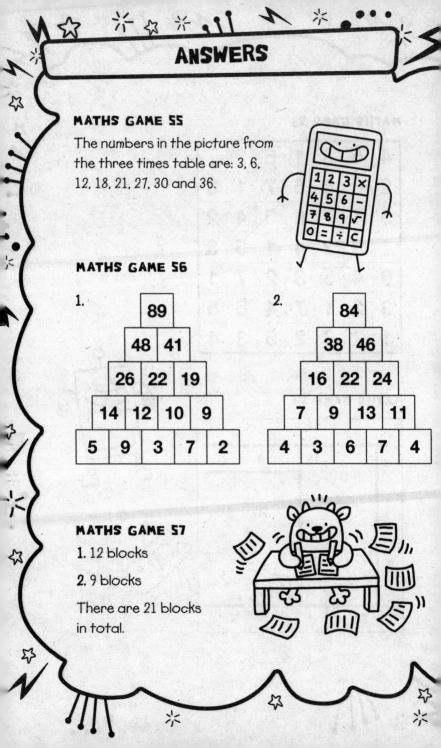

MATHS GAME 55

The numbers in the picture from the three times table are: 3, 6, 12, 18, 21, 27, 30 and 36.

MATHS GAME 56

1.

		89		
	48	41		
	26	22	19	
14	12	10	9	
5	9	3	7	2

2.

		84		
	38	46		
	16	22	24	
7	9	13	11	
4	3	6	7	4

MATHS GAME 57

1. 12 blocks

2. 9 blocks

There are 21 blocks in total.

MATHS GAME 58

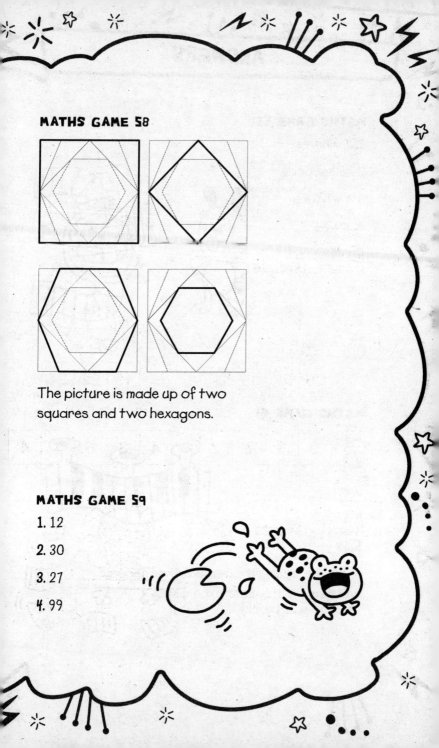

The picture is made up of two squares and two hexagons.

MATHS GAME 59

1. 12
2. 30
3. 27
4. 99

ANSWERS

MATHS GAME 60

1. 2 minutes
2. 45 seconds
3. 1 ½ hours
4. 3 weeks
5. 25 hours

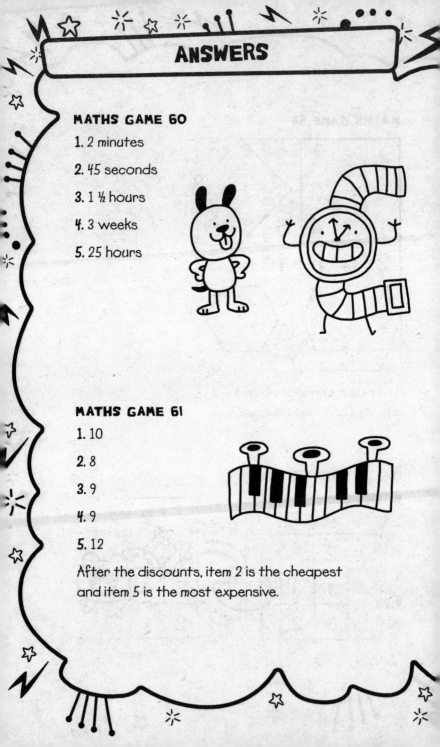

MATHS GAME 61

1. 10
2. 8
3. 9
4. 9
5. 12

After the discounts, item 2 is the cheapest and item 5 is the most expensive.

MATHS GAME 62

4	3	1	2	5	6
5	6	3	4	1	2
1	2	4	6	3	5
2	5	6	1	4	3
6	1	5	3	2	4
3	4	2	5	6	1

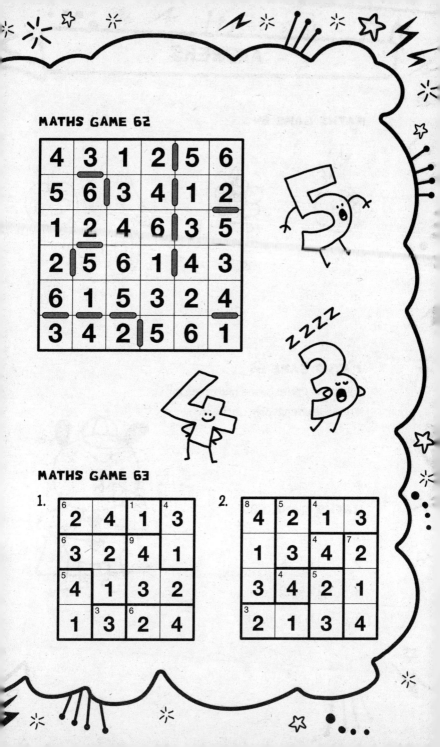

MATHS GAME 63

1.

6		1	4
2	4	1	3
3	2	4	1
4	1	3	2
1	3	2	4

With cage clues: 6, 1, 4 (top row); 6, 9 (second row); 5 (third row); 3, 6 (fourth row).

2.

8	5	4	
4	2	1	3
1	3	4	2
3	4	2	1
2	1	3	4

With cage clues: 8, 5, 4 (top row); 4, 7 (second row); 4, 5 (third row); 3 (fourth row).

ANSWERS

MATHS GAME 64

 = 4   = 6   = 2   = 1

MATHS GAME 65

All the numbers are multiples of three, except 854 and 136.

MATHS GAME 66

1. 3+11 = 14
2. 3+4+11 = 18
3. 4+9+12 = 25
4. 8+9+11+12 = 40

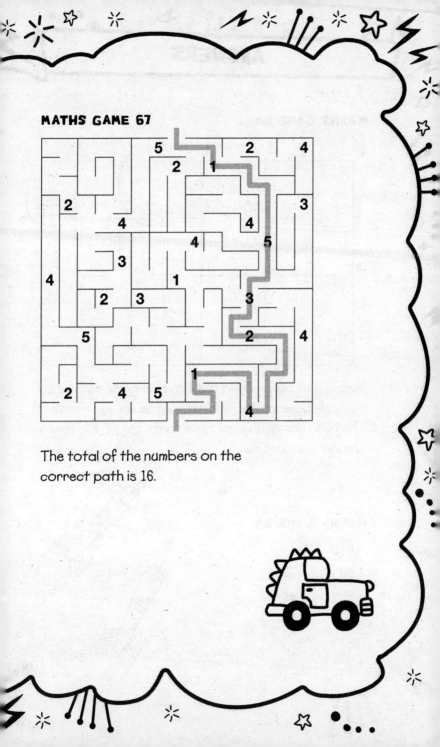

MATHS GAME 67

The total of the numbers on the
correct path is 16.

MATHS GAME 68

7		2	4		3			2		2

(grid with numbers)

3 | 2 | 1

3 | | 2 | 1

2 | | 1

2 | | 1

Keep count by working out how many rectangles can be made by each top-left corner, as shown above. Then you can add up all the counts to get the final answer, which is 35.

MATHS GAME 69

1. 21 + 2 = 23

2. 23 + 10 = 33

3. 21 + 13 = 34

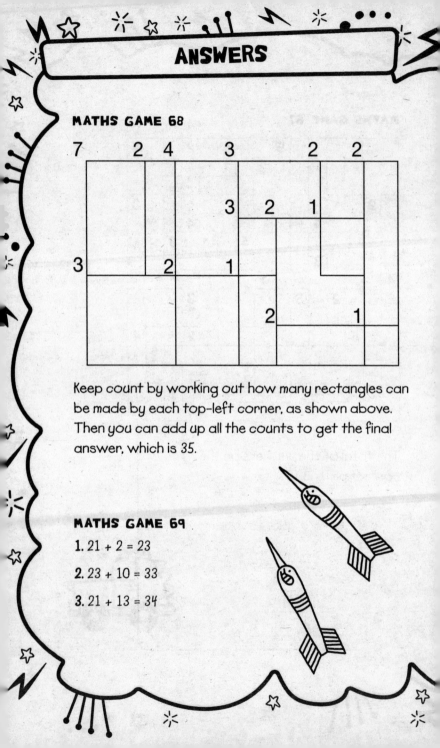

MATHS GAME 70

1. 7 x 2 (= 14) changed to 16 – 1 (= 15)

2. 10 x 5 (= 50) changed to 55 – 10 (= 45)

3. 8 + 7 (= 15) changed to 5 + 9 (= 14)

4. 13 + 37 (= 50) changed to 39 + 12 (= 51)

5. 150 + 5 (= 155) changed to 160 – 10 (= 150)

The locations of the changed sums are numbered in the picture below. The five differences to the picture are also circled below.

ANSWERS

MATHS GAME 71

1.

4		2		3		1
2		1		4		3
^						
3		4		1		2
v		v		^		
1		3	>	2		4

2.

2		1		3		4
				^		
1	<	2		4		3
3		4		1		2
		v				
4		3	>	2	>	1

MATHS GAME 72

1. – 12
2. + 6
3. – 4
4. × 2

MATHS GAME 73

1. 55
2. 39
3. 60
4. 28

MATHS GAME 74

1. 8.45 p.m.
2. 11.00 a.m.
3. 5.10 p.m.
4. 5.30 a.m.
5. 12.50 p.m.

MATHS GAME 75

1. 4 coins: 10z + 1z + 1z + 1z

2. 4 coins: 50z + 20z + 10z + 5z

3. 3 coins: 10z + 5z + 1z (16z change from 60z paid)

MATHS GAME 76

🧁		1	2	🧁
2		🧁	4	2
🧁	3	🧁	🧁	1
2		3		2
🧁	2	🧁	2	🧁

MATHS GAME 77

1. 51: add 3 at each step

2. 102: subtract 8 at each step

3. 67: add 9 at each step

4. 1: divide by 2 at each step

MATHS GAME 78

1.

	3	7	7	3	
4	1	3	4	2	6
6	2	4	3	1	4
4	3	1	2	4	6
6	4	2	1	3	4
	7	3	3	7	

2.

	6	4	6	4	
3	2	1	4	3	7
7	4	3	2	1	3
7	3	4	1	2	3
3	1	2	3	4	7
	4	6	4	6	

MATHS GAME 79

1.

4 3	6 2	4	9 5	1
1	3 3	13 2	4	7 5
7 5	4	1	3	2
2	6 5	3	1 1	7 4
4 4	1	7 5	2	3

2.

5 1	8 3	5	6 2	4
4	1 1	9 2	3	8 5
8 5	11 2	1 1	4	3
3	5	4	1 1	3 2
6 2	4	8 3	5	1

ANSWERS

MATHS GAME 80

1.

```
        88
      47  41
    24  23  18
  11  13  10  8
 5   6   7   3   5
4   1   5   2   1   4
```

2.

```
        83
      47  36
    27  20  16
  15  12  8   8
 7   8   4   4   4
2   5   3   1   3   1
```

MATHS GAME 81

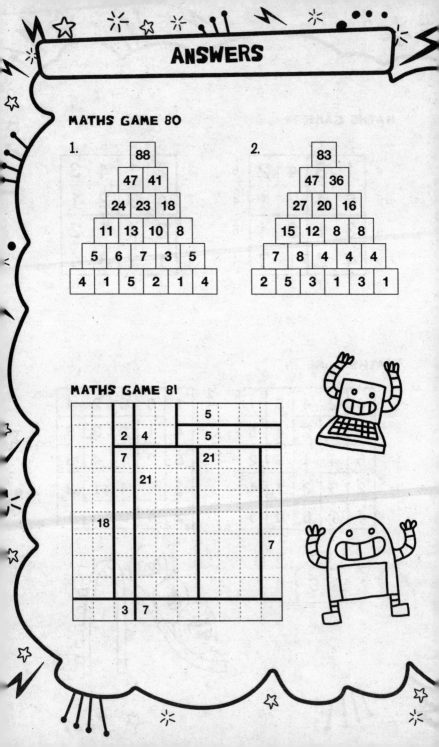

				5	
	2	4		5	
	7		21		
		21			
18					
					7
	3	7			

MATHS GAME 82

1. $11 + 2 + 1 = 14$

2. $13 + 2 + 6 = 21$

3. $9 + 15 + 6 = 30$

MATHS GAME 83

3	4	2	5	6	1
5	2	1	6	3	4
6	3	4	1	2	5
1	6	5	3	4	2
4	5	3	2	1	6
2	1	6	4	5	3

NOTES AND SCRIBBLES

NOTES

NOTES

NOTES

NOTES

NOTES

NOTES

ALSO AVAILABLE:

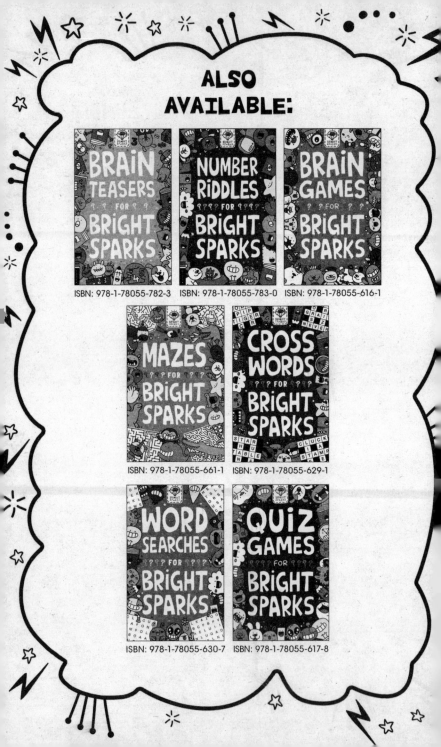